INTO THE BLUE FAR DISTANCE

Dear Connie,

As our "earth mother" all those years, you deserve credit for having helped me see the reasons for some — and coming back. Share this with our other friends. And thanks for everything.

Love,

INTO THE BLUE FAR DISTANCE

MEMORIES AND MUSING FROM AMERICA'S ROADS

Michael W. Burns

Writers Club Press
New York Lincoln Shanghai

Into The Blue Far Distance
Memories and Musing from America's Roads

Writers Club Press
an imprint of iUniverse, Inc.

For information address:
iUniverse
2021 Pine Lake Road, Suite 100
Lincoln, NE 68512
www.iuniverse.com

ISBN: 0-595-25346-6 (Pbk)
ISBN: 0-595-65111-9 (Cloth)

Printed in the United States of America

"Carry Away My Soul Into The Blue Far Distance"

From a Latvian Folk song

This book is dedicated to all those who have found themselves facing extraordinary circumstances yet have managed to live an ordinary life.

That is all I have tried to do.

ACKNOWLEDGEMENT

This is a work of nonfiction, the historical data that appears in the text is information gathered by word of mouth, visitor center brochures or the websites of the states and communities through which I passed. All of the places are real as are the people. The names off certain towns have been left out intentionally as have the names of certain people. It was done because all the information about them is in the public domain. I also did not want to identify the towns that I spent time visiting in some cases since it might embarrass those who provided information to me. The information is true so far as I am aware but I have taken the word of the person who provided it to me and have not researched it. In my view, it did not require identification or footnoting.

None of the individuals who are named are fictitious. I either did not ever know their full names or have chosen not to use them since I do not believe it is critical to the story.

I wish to thank all those who helped in this effort. Particular thanks go to my wife Joanne, who had the confidence to let me go and to suffer the writing of this book, and to my nephew William Burns of YOFI Productions in Denver, CO, who gave so selflessly of his time in maintaining the website, www.thevictorylap.com which made the journey come alive for me and the many who followed it. He provided much more than just technical support.

I thank and acknowledge all those who maintain and update some very informative websites for many communities and nearly all states. I would suggest that if any reader wishes to learn more about some of the places in this book, that these sites would be a wonderful place to start.

CONTENTS

FOREWORD XV

APRIL

DEPARTURE 1
ONE
    ARIZONA AND LAS CRUCES, NEW MEXICO 4
TWO
    ROSWELL, NEW MEXICO 11
THREE
    AMARILLO, TEXAS 14
FOUR
    SHAMROCK TEXAS, OKLAHOMA CITY AND KEYSTONE STATE
    PARK 20
FIVE
    A TOWN IN OKLAHOMA, A TOWN IN TWO STATES, PARIS,
    AND A PLACE CALLED HOPE 24
SIX
    "SWINGING BRIDGE", JACKSON, MISSISSIPPI 34
SEVEN
    PENSACOLA, FLORIDA 42
EIGHT
    GADSDEN, ALABAMA 54
NINE
    PIGEON FORGE AT KNOXVILLE, TENNESSEE 59
TEN
    SMOKY MOUNTAIN NATIONAL PARK 64

MAY

ELEVEN
    LOST AND FOUND IN THE CAROLINAS 71
TWELVE
    THE BLUE RIDGE PARKWAY 75
THIRTEEN
    WINCHESTER, VIRGINIA;
    GETTYSBURG, AND A LADY NAMED DOT 81
FOURTEEN
    LEBANON AND
    THE LACKAWANNA VALLEY 90
FIFTEEN
    COOPERSTOWN, GLIMMERGLASS, ...95
    AND A PLACE CALLED
    ROTTERDAM 95
SIXTEEN
    MEMORIAL DAY, JEFFERSON, MASSACHUSETTS 106

JUNE

SEVENTEEN
    CONNECTICUT BY THE SEA 111
EIGHTEEN
    TENAFLY 115
NINETEEN
    POINT PLEASANT 122
TWENTY
    WASHINGTON, D.C. 126
TWENTY-ONE
    BEDFORD, BUTLER, AND THE LINCOLN HIGHWAY 137
TWENTY-TWO
    MILAN, OHIO 142

TWENTY-THREE
  MICHIGAN AND ILLINOIS 149
TWENTY-FOUR
  THE BIRTHPLACE OF "DUTCH"; A FIELD OF DREAMS;
  AND LOOKING FOR RADAR O'REILLY 152
TWENTY-FIVE
  YANKTON, SOUTH DAKOTA 157
TWENTY-SIX
  DEADWOOD, CRAZY HORSE, AND MOUNT RUSHMORE 163
TWENTY-SEVEN
  WHEATLAND, WYOMING 169

JULY

TWENTY-EIGHT
  FORT COLLINS AND DENVER, COLORADO 172
TWENTY-NINE
  COLORADO AND UTAH 176
THIRTY
  COMING HOME 182

EPILOGUE 187

FOREWORD

The idea did not come overnight. For more than thirty years I had dreamt of this journey. It was the one I had promised I would take when I left military service. Unfortunately, the way I left made it impossible. I thought then it would never be taken. The idea stayed with me, but life also got in the way. The ordinary things like work, marriage, the DMV, taxes, mortgages, a headache, and all the other mundane matters of living deferred the dream. But I did not forget it.

More than 30 years later I had the opportunity and the vehicle to do it. The opportunity came as I retired from federal service and before I went on to other things. I had finished a career not many had bet I would have, and I owed myself an adventure. Since any new opportunities were at least six months away, I had the time to do whatever I wanted until then.

I also found the vehicle. I had lulled myself to sleep more than once over the years trying to envision a floor plan for a van. It had to be small enough to be driven like a car, parked like a car and handle pretty much like one as well, but it had to have all the things in it I would need to lead a "self-contained" life. It needed a bed, of course, a refrigerator and a bath and it also had to be large enough for me to move around in a wheelchair. I did not want a "Motor Coach" of 35 feet. I really had no desire to learn to drive a "bus" around residential streets and in and out of the parking lots of restaurants; I just wanted something in which I could carry everything I needed and sleep.

xvi / Into The Blue Far Distance

About two years before I retired, I saw a magazine article that pic-
tured a van of the correct size and other characteristics that was being
manufactured by a company in Canada, Leisure Vans Ltd., called the
"Independence." In time I inquired of them as to whether they had a
dealer near me and found that there was one an hour or so north. I did
nothing with the information until one day six or eight months before I
retired but after I had decided to do so. I mentioned it to my Physical
Therapist while she was trying to make my neck less sore again. She was
enthusiastic about it, and curious for her other patients as well. We saw
it and quickly figured out that this thing would probably work. I had
never been in anything like it before. I had never been inside any type of
Motor Home and was completely ignorant of how all the systems
worked. It seemed incredibly complicated. It was a car and a house all in
one. But, since there are millions of these, much larger than the one I
purchased driven by folks certainly no smarter than I, it seemed possible to figure it out.

I now possessed an efficiency apartment. It was but 20 feet long and
7 feet wide, yet had everything I could need, including a microwave
oven. I mastered driving it in a four day trip up the California coast in
January and a trip to Las Vegas to see friends and Phoenix in March to
visit with my brother at what is becoming our annual baseball spring
training trip. I found that what I bought for the mere convenience of
not having to try to maneuver around an inaccessible house or motel
was actually a nice quiet place in which I seemed to enjoy living. Best of
all, the design I had dreamt about had been done for me and, on the
whole, it worked. I certainly didn't mind the small hook-up fees I had to
pay the campsites in order to get "on" the electric, water and sewage systems. It could also operate self-contained, so the driveways of my
friends and relatives could serve as parking places as well.

I have not survived life in a wheelchair through spontaneity. To get
up, to go to work and to get through the day required self-discipline and
a daily plan that had to be adhered to rigorously. I was now planning to

xvii / Michael W. Burns

drive east, north, south and west again to a new place nearly everyday, eating in new restaurants and meeting new people. I had no idea what I was going to find in the next three months. I had never even tried such a thing before, and I intended to do all of it alone. After years of certainty in my daily life, none of this seemed to concern me. I am not sure why. It appeared to be the chance of a lifetime to take a "Victory Lap" around the United States. It seemed that if you did it one day at a time, had faith in yourself, your resourcefulness and the kindness of strangers, it would not be hard.

The look in the eyes of those who saw me packing the van to go reminded me of John Steinbeck's conversations with his neighbors before he left on his fabled trip with his dog Charlie. They get a distant look; some even express a desire to be able go along. It is, and he put it far better than this, the chance to be on the road with no schedule and in no hurry with all you will need to survive.

-2-

The getting ready may be harder than the going. This micro version of my house and all those things that one needs to live in it must be packed. Things need to have some logic in where they are stored in the van. It has a great deal of storage, but if it isn't organized, I think I could spend the better part of the day just looking for things. I like to think of parts of it as "areas of influence." The back is for sleeping, mostly, but also for storage under the floor. This is for things you won't need everyday. The kitchen is to the left. The bath is to the right and the closet as well. Forward of that, above the doors and windows, are open storage racks for things you made need while driving, or in a hurry after you stop. Over the driver and passengers seats there is more storage for things you will use when that area becomes your "living room" for the night. The TV, VCR and CD player are all there. There are curtains, too, that cover the windshield, to close up the house for the night.

Outside, on each side, there are "cubbies"; spaces with locking doors that house a tool box, or a space to put water bottles, the electric and water connections. Each one that is only for storage is placed in a way to be convenient to the task one might perform near there. A water hose and the gloves and spare parts are logically near where the service for electricity and water is located, while the toolbox is on the other side near the door.

Just getting it put together for a trip of 60 days, and then remembering where it all is, tests the memory. One of the standing jokes on the trip when I had misplaced something was that "it was in the van." It was like a very large suitcase in that way. Once, a grommet that belonged in the refrigerator door hinge got lost somehow. There is a rule of inevitability in moving micro homes: All things will eventually roll to the front unless constrained from doing so. One afternoon, ten or 20 days into the trip, I found the grommet near the drivers seat and put it in a container I had for loose things that showed up at the end of the day. My brother and I put it back in when I got to Michigan a month later. It had not affected the performance of the refrigerator and I knew it had to be in the van. A pair of sweatpants disappeared early in the trip in one of the storage compartments. I found them when I got home. So "its in the van" could mean anything that I was sure I knew I could not find, but that I knew would eventually appear.

The "house" has to move every day, so plans to secure things need to be made, otherwise the van can quickly fill with unguided missiles. Enough things will shake loose on a bad road without any help, so "screwing" everything down before you leave home, and knowing how you will lash it down every morning becomes important. Doing it with some speed is essential when you are trying to get back on the road.

The "preflight" of planning how far you will drive and where you will stay gets pretty intense, particularly when you try to leave time in places you think you will want to visit. This gets to be even more tortuous when you have never driven the route before. After some trial and error, and the realization that unless you know how much you have to go up and down hill, the solution seemed to be to plan no more than two weeks at a time and do the rest as you went along. There are too many variables to be very efficient. I planned a route to Pensacola, Florida. The rest will get worked out later. It was harder work than loading the van. Campsites were called to ascertain their accessibility to my wheelchair, and their availability on a specific day. A more comprehensive plan would be far too compulsive for this trip. I will, however, make every effort to be off the road on weekends when most of the "pleasure drivers" are abundant.

It is easy to say that you will live with no schedule and be in no hurry, as I have said I would many times, but it quickly becomes apparent that even casual travelers have some schedule and occasionally have to hurry. Or, as my Father used to say, likely in another context, "Everyone's gotta be somewhere."

I had seen enough of the desert and its' heat for one year, but to leave this part of the "Left Coast" and go east, you must go through it. I plan my route to try to minimize the time I will be in it. I know it will be boring and I can only hope it will not yet be too hot. I will head east to Pensacola, Florida and turn left, head north and hope to be at the entrance to the Great Smoky Mountain National Park by early May. The stops for now are to be one night in Arizona, Las Cruces, NM, on to Roswell NM, where I will look for UFOs, of course. I will continue on U.S. 70 to what I am told to be a lovely state park near Amarillo TX (known as the "Grand Canyon of Texas") for my first two day stop. I have a side trip to Enid Oklahoma planned, for no other reason than it is a common four letter word in crossword puzzles for a town in Oklahoma. I also think I promised someone I would visit the main street there for some reason, but I do not recall who it was. The route then goes and on to Tulsa OK. Going this way has me driving as few miles in Texas as possible. This may or may not be a political statement, but it does say a great deal about my distaste for dry heat, wind, and the kind of dust storms that can take the paint right off your car. Texarkana, which is in two states, is next (and a side trip to Hope, Arkansas). Then it is on to Jackson Mississippi for two days and to Pensacola for three. The Navy made an officer and a gentleman of me there. It also has very large Naval Aviation Museum there now I want to see.

I will turn left, and head north to travel the Blue Ridge Parkway to Front Royal, Virginia where it ends.

If I get to Vermont, I will make a U-turn and come back to the Boston area, New Jersey, Washington DC, and then head west to Michigan, Chicago, the upper Midwest and on to Denver by early July. I will then take a very deep breath and see if I have time and energy to go further before the real vacationers hit the road, or whether it will be time to head for home. It is an ambitious trip, and it all may change in the first week.

Any further planning and I may never leave. Packing the van is a bit like cleaning the garage. Remembering things not easily bought, like wheelchair spare parts, is a challenge. But that is why FedEx was invented. Something will be left behind, but as my sister-in-law reminds me, there is a Wal-Mart nearly everywhere. What you don't remember can always be bought.

DEPARTURE

"He who is outside his door already has the hard part of his journey behind him."

A Dutch Proverb

My home of the last sixteen years is now a speck in the rear view mirror. My journey has begun in the dark of an April morning when the dew is heavy and there is a chill in the air. It is an ambivalent time, as I contemplate leaving that warm place of last night for the uncertainty of today tomorrow and many days to come.

Somewhere in my mind there are thoughts of how this journey will be. I tell myself to have an open mind, to care only about what may come as I make the next turn or go around the next bend in the road. I want to be surprised and delight in a new discovery, I want to find the world new and fresh and wondrous and funny as a child would find it. I want at least to give myself the chance to have those feelings and reactions to what I see and experience for the next 3 months.

It is, as I head south for the desert and first light, a contemplative moment. I do not worry about what I may need and have left behind and I do not worry about what may be ahead. There will be, if life runs true, some very good things, some boredom and some frightening moments. When I was flying, we used to have a saying about how it was hours of boredom interspersed with moments of sheer terror. I think about this trip as moments of boredom, interspersed with hours of wonder, humor and peace. Thinking of what can go wrong now will not

1

make it less likely to occur. I am content to follow the slower traffic down the freeway before heading east in the first light listening to a voice on the radio I have always enjoyed and will not hear for a while. I am enjoying the thought that I have all day to go any distance and I may stop and do other things if I wish or not. There is a world of possibilities that await me and I will meet as many as I can as time goes by. I will see people I have never seen, others I have not seen in many years and family I wish to re-connect with before they are too old to remember or I am gone and they are not. I wish to see the children of these people, to enjoy them while both they and I are not yet too old to be joyful. To miss this stage of their lives is a thing I would hate, for it is to these little people that I feel close. Perhaps there is some truth to the theory that the older we get the more we identify with the very young. I am a man without a schedule aside from what my body may dictate, as are they. I see things as new as they do everyday and marvel at them as they do as well. We have a lot in common; the "wee people" and I, and I know that I will enjoy this trip if I can let this sense of wonder run free.

There are really two parts to this journey. I am out here, alone, experiencing the wonder of the world and the bad things as well. There will be long stretches, such as this first one of more than two weeks when I will speak to not one living soul that I know. Some would be uncomfortable with that. I am not. Perhaps I am naive about those I will meet. Another part will be with friends and family that will bring back memories and produce conversations that will move and amuse me but will not be entirely new. I look forward to that part greatly because these people I will see are important to me. What they think and feel now in there lives is different from what they felt when we last met. It will be a wondrous time to know how they have grown, or not, and changed, or not. It is an opportunity that I cherish and perhaps what inspired the trip in the first place. Some of these people are now in the prime of they're working years and spend much time with their jobs and then have time for family when they can. I will miss some of them because of this scheduled life they lead. I am sure the children and I will have more time to spend together than the parents. I know that there will be things I will miss but cannot regret them now or when I do. There will be people that I miss but I cannot regret that now or if I do. Those things and those people will not intersect with me this time around. I do not worry about it now since there is nothing I can do about it. I will try to schedule my way into their busy lives when they can best be interrupted, for the children and I are the ones with time and flexibility on our side.

I am pleased to be going, which means that the adventure that I believe is out there is greater than the force that would hold me back. I hope that I will have the same enthusiasm for it, and the desire to chronicle it, when it is near an end as I do as it begins.

As the sun rises and I turn east, I move toward an unknown road full of unmet people. It is a world of new experiences, and a trip like none I have ever taken to places I have never been, or have not been for a very long time.

I know it will be a memory forever.

ONE

ARIZONA AND LAS CRUCES, NEW MEXICO

There are mountains to cross between San Diego and Yuma Arizona. Then the land turns flat and I endure the tedium and heat of the very southern part of Arizona. There are those who believe Interstate 8 from Yuma AZ to the junction with I-10 is the hottest and most boring highway in the world. I will give it my vote as the worst in the southwest. It is, in all respects, a reason why talking books were invented. I had lunch in Gila Bend. Aside from the very nice truck stop and the café I ate in, there is precious little in Gila Bend on a day near 100 degrees to attract interest. Perhaps there is something here that would attract me in midwinter but not now. The café is said to be on the site of what was a "bustling" stagecoach trail. The place and its attendant gasoline and diesel pumps still bustle. The town's Chamber of Commerce boasts of nine months of "exquisite" climate. This is clearly not one of them. They also assure me they are a full service community, otherwise undefined.

There are three kinds of cacti that I recognize along the road here. I know the name of one, the Saguaro, which is the one that looks to me like someone in a moment of perpetual surrender since the two "arms" are raised skyward. Near Tucson you can see a whole monument devoted to them. There are acres and acres of them, some 15 feet tall. They only flower a few hours at night for two months of the year, but provide an enormous amount of water storage for what little wildlife there is. The archives tell of thousands that were cut down as the state was developed since no one really appreciated the need to preserve them then. The small, night blooming flower is the Official State Flower now in appreciation of the wondrous nature of such a bit of flora. There is also a very portly one with no branches that flower nicely in the spring. There is another spindly one that blooms yellow even this late. It doesn't even look much like a cactus. Most of the ones along the stretch are sorry specimens, which have holes everywhere that have been hammered by birds either for water or a nesting place. These now resemble Swiss cheese. There appear to be more holes than Cacti. Once you have seen the three species a few hundred times, you begin to try to find almost anything else to look at along the way. The "washes", for example, which is what they call the dry creek beds, since when it rains here, it washes through, sometimes with great ferocity but doesn't stay wet long. There are many small bridges that span these creeks and "Rios." Most all have a name. Most all the names are Spanish. Now and then there is one that proclaims river status and the bridge is a bit longer and the sand bed below a bit wider. I have only traveled this road once in the rain. It is certain that you would not travel it at all in those times were it not for these many bridges, some only five or ten feet off the bed of the wash. The water would simply overflow onto the road. They just get wider, not deeper, unless the storm is truly bad. In an attempt to amuse, you count them, and then try to calculate the cost added to the road so that the flood that comes once or twice a year would not close the road. You grind along this virtually deserted Interstate on the way east. Another car or a truck seen is almost a reason to rejoice here in the middle of the day. I suppose I should be buying acreage along here right now, because there is no doubt if they can get water as Phoenix did, this too will become part of the Arizona winter playground.

There are few gas stops to speak of, just enough to get people where they are going. There are many abandoned diners and gas pumps along the road, indicating that speculators thought this route would be the one of choice, rather than Interstate 10 to the north. That one goes through Phoenix and the greener part of the state. Unfortunately for the speculators, anyone coming out of Los Angeles and north finds it far more convenient. Only two lane roads connect it to this desolate place. Perhaps there were other roads planned to connect them. These fossilized stations, restaurants, and the occasion shell of a motel are the remnants of the entrepreneurial spirit that came with the original construction. They have a charm, but since I have traveled this way many times, it is not one that I find easy to recall.

Remarkably, from one of the on ramps there appears an exact replica of my van, right down to the handicapped license plate. Had his plate not been from Arizona, I would have thought it a mirage. There are not many Leisure Travel Vans seen in this part of the United States and certainly not very many that are adapted for handicapped use. As I draw closer, I see that his doors are not extra high as mine are to allow you to move from the lift into the van without ducking your head every time. That is about the only difference; even the paint is the same. I wave as I go by and am met with thumbs up from the driver and a wave from his passenger. I get the feeling he is trying to talk to me on the CB radio, which, by the large antennae, I can tell he clearly has. I only have an emergency set which has no reception in the van when it is running so I keep going with another wave. There may be brotherhood of Leisure Van owners, but it is small since they sell more vans in Canada than they do in the United States. This is in fact the last I see until I am on my way into Chicago in another two months.

Picacho State Park, between Phoenix and Tucson, is my first overnight stop. It has spectacular views from a mesa high above the desert floor with caves even higher. It was the highlight of the day and a nice place to stop. Legend says that the Indians came to these mesas that I am camping among tonight because it got cool early in the day since the sun set behind them. There may also have been water in the caves.

The sunset and sunrise I saw were spectacular. The Ranger told me that it was 98 degrees when I arrived. I guess he thought I needed to know that. I felt a lot warmer after he mentioned it. There was only one other camper in the vehicle area, but lots of "tenters" further up the trails. There are only electrical hook-ups here. This is typical of U.S. and state parks. Some have facilities to dump off used water on the way out so that the weight of the vehicle can be reduced. I managed to make an awkward hookup in the blistering dry heat. All they have really done here for campers is put power in a parking lot that didn't get much use. They put the power stanchions up on the curb and far enough away that I had to go down the paved lot to a curb ramp and up on the walk and back again. It was not possible to reach the power outlet from the street. This dry heat is that which my body likes the least, so it made the routine difficult. I quickly learned that the air conditioning worked and also spent the first hour with a wet towel over my head trying to cool down while I drank about two liters of water. After the sun had crested, I went out and said hello to my only neighbor. He was retired and lived in the Phoenix area so they were not a long way from home. I met his mother and his wife who was along for the night to "exercise" his 35 foot RV, and had a pleasant conversation before dinner. I suppose I heard first names, but I do not remember them and doubt any of us thought that very important.

I did get to turn off the air conditioning that night when 30-knot wind gusts came up. It was like being aboard ship again. Rocked me right to sleep even if it was noisy. It even rained for about ten minutes, quite lovely all in all.

-2-

I ate a quiet breakfast while watching my neighbors walk their dogs. I waved to them as I went back out on the Interstate into what I knew would be another hot day in search of Las Cruces New Mexico. Getting out of the dessert was my mission. After crossing the Rio Grande River and traveling on into Las Cruces it improved. The town is interesting for its' history and I wish I'd more time to spend here. Of course, I could have made the time, but I was still in that part of the trip where getting where I said I would go had some meaning to me, when there really was no reason at all. So except for the local visitors center and a few sights on the way to the campground, there was a lot I missed.

This is another of the "frontier towns" where the border is not very important. Crossing it means little to the inhabitants of either side. It is difficult to even know how the town was named. Some say it is merely a Spanish translation for crossroads. Others have more elaborate theories. One has it that a Bishop and a Priest were traveling with a Mexican Army Colonel and captain and four choir boys and they were attacked near the Rio Grande and all were killed but one boy that survived. Crosses were erected in their honor and the name, *El Pueblo del Jardin de Las Cruces* (the City of the Garden of Crosses) evolved and then was shortened. Much of this area's history is tied to the Gadsden Purchase, which was a small piece of land—by Louisiana Purchase standards—which the U.S. purchased in 1854 from Mexico. It was 30,000 square miles, bought for $10 million dollars, generally taking most land north and west of the Rio Grande under U.S. rule. There was a new bustling village growing quickly on the west side of the river called *Dona Ana,* which was established at the end of the U.S. War with Mexico. They preferred being Mexican so much that they moved the whole new village to the west side of the river when the treaty that ended the war placed them in U.S. territory.

Sadly, when the Gadsden Purchase was completed six years later, they were back in the U.S. without having moved at all. Most of them stayed in their new village named for the fact that it was on a hill (*mesita*). It was called Mesilla. They were never very happy about all this as one might suspect, so they never considered themselves under U.S. rule and lived out their lives as though still citizens of Mexico. This area is no stranger to ethnic and nationalistic tensions.

All these border areas have similar stories. Most are confusing. No one is sure which is true. The Mexicans usually prefer one version and the New Mexico residents the other. Between the Treaty of Guadalupe Hidalgo that formerly ended the so called Mexican America War which was finalized in 1848 and the Purchase some six years later, it all gets as muddy as the Rio Grande after a rain storm.

The Siesta Campground was a pleasant place. A young couple, émigrés from New Jersey of all places, runs it. In another life he had been an unhappy plant manager. He is now a happy campground owner, and a very funny man. This is a place that is "eastern Arizona" for many winter snowbirds. The campgrounds such as these thrive on seasonal travelers. While I was there, he was kind enough to let me use his computer to exchange my mail. He took a call, which he said filled him up for the season. I must have looked confused because he gently explained that he meant the coming winter.

My visit was short, only overnight, but I was grateful for the 57 degree temperature and the nice people. I figured I was making progress when I saw pine trees here in the valley. For pine trees you need water, so this seemed a harbinger of cooler, less desert like weather. Unfortunately the eerie sight of the white sand dunes an hour east and 2000 feet higher in elevation soon changed all that.

As I readied to leave in the morning, I found, for reasons that made no sense at all, that the ignition key had been on all night and my engine battery was dead. My new friend the owner responded to my call on the cell phone since the ramp on the van operates on that battery only. All the appliances in the rear have separate power. Since I had yet to have a reason to go outside, I had no idea that I couldn't. He brought his pickup truck and jump-started it. My shamefaced embarrassment earned me the right to leave without having to pay for it. I sense that this will not be the last act of kindness by a complete stranger that will make my trip both possible and interesting. At least I waited until my second day to do something that stupid. Had I been in that sparsely inhabited public campground in Arizona, I would have had to try to hunt down a Ranger and call AAA to jump-start the van. I suppose it means two things: I am very lucky, and from this day on I will take the keys from the ignition before I go to bed.

Onward.

TWO

ROSWELL, NEW MEXICO

Welcome to Roswell, NM, which, according to the local Chamber of Commerce, is on the list of " Ten Towns Worth Calling Home." The Chamber alleges it is an affordable place with low taxes, a diverse economy and a wonderful climate.

Well.

It is the home of The International UFO Museum and Research Center. It is 90 degrees today. It is very dusty. It will rain tonight, thunderstorms, and in order to get here from the west you have to pass through the White Sands Missile Test Area where the people are less friendly than they have been in or near any place I have ever called home. In order to get here, you pass the place they dropped the first atomic bomb. While historic and intellectually interesting, it might depress me if I had to pass it on my way "home" very often. They are close to U.S. 70 (which is how you get 'home") whenever they fire a missile. The good news is there was none scheduled until next week so I did not need to wait the two or more hours in the local coffee shops (they must live for such things) while they did whatever it is they do during a firing sequence. U.S. 70's further charm is that it remains the main street of Roswell. There are no familiar "U.S. 70 Business" signs with a bypass. I suppose it improves business and terminates the argument of whether stores should relocate to the highway, but at the end of a day of driving in the heat, watching for parked cars pulling out is not a pleasant circumstance in a strange town. It may well be a nice place, but it has more oddities than I would care to have in my "home" just to lower my taxes a bit.

In July of 1947 (in the first half of the last century, for you young folks) an article was published in the local paper here about aliens and the visits certain locals had made to the "mother ships" that came by night. The Army Air Corps, of course, took an immediate interest and sent some Public Information Officer to see what was up. He ended up being convinced by one Glenn Dennis, who worked in the local funeral home, that he had indeed visited with the aliens and an industry was born. That is the Roswell I know about. I am sure that there is more to it than that, but that is what I have seen and what the people talk about. It seems the Chamber of Commerce is more interested in overcoming the "negative" stories about this strange place than they are in exploiting it. After all, the U.S. Government has never said that UFO's do not exist; they simply say that they haven't seen them.

To keep my options open, however, I am in a motel tonight. If the van gets beamed up, I guess I rent a car in the morning. Actually, the accommodations were nice; the Mexican food (that was me downing the Enchiladas and refries in "Juano's" next door to the motel) was very good. I used the evening to answer e-mail on the now almost universal data jacks found in motel rooms and add a note to the web page about the adventures so far. I enjoy the spacious room and the capacious bed. It reminds me of what was called "hotel night" when I was in the Navy. It was the night before the sheets got sent to the laundry so some took the opportunity to sleep in the bed (that is between the sheets) instead of on top of them as we did the rest of the week since it was impossible to make a bunk the way that would please your Gunnery Sergeant in the four minutes you had to get ready for inspection.

I miss sleeping in the van. I am not sure whether I should be happy about that, but I accept it as so. I do very much enjoy the luxury of too many towels I will not have to wash and the hot shower even more.

Tomorrow it is on to Amarillo, or more accurately, Pablo Duro Canyon State Park near Canyon, Texas. Amarillo is about one hundred miles north. This is a two-day "rest" stop if it works out. It is the first of many state parks planned along the way, but, since I have no idea what that means in terms of access, accommodations or scenery, I will learn from this stay. The state of Texas, like others, has a centralized campsite reservation service. You can dial an 800 number and they will give you a specific site in any of their parks for specific dates. You can even pay the fee and they will tell you what the park has as services and attractions. It makes things simple for the traveler, particularly when trying to get weekend nights. I have tried to book reservations for Friday and Saturday, or Saturday and Sunday from here through Tennessee to be off the road on weekends. These are the times when the sites are most heavily used, so "drive up" traffic doesn't fare too well, particularly if the weather forecast is good. This Park has a website, as many do, and is where I learned it is the "Grand Canyon of Texas."

Leaving Roswell reasonably early I am greeted with the sight of a hot air balloon following the main road. Anything airborne that looks odd in this town draws your attention. I suppose flying a hot air balloon at 8 o'clock in the morning along the general path of U.S. 70, is not unusual here. It seems a fitting end to my stay in the place that is described in fairly serious literature as one that "may have been visited by aliens."

THREE

AMARILLO, TEXAS

The trip here continued along U.S. 70. It crossed the flatlands of New Mexico and Texas where some of the largest cattle feed lots exist, as do some very small towns. Clovis, NM would be the largest of these and looks pretty much like the place everyone would be on a Saturday night. Sorry I missed Saturday night in Clovis. I bet it is a real hoot. This is a country of ranches, too, with free-ranging horses. There are real cowboys here. I have seen them riding, moving a herd of horses across open range. It is a sight that is leaving the landscape. Perhaps that is why it is even more beautiful. These are the cowboys Willie Nelson sings about. They are dying breed, but the sight of these large, strong men moving horses, or driving a feed truck up the road before dusk is still one that inspires dreams and fantasies, and a variety of country songs. It is what makes them special; the reputation for living hard, working hard, and dying young is still a part of them, even in the 21st Century. To watch two run a herd several miles, keeping them together and all headed in the right direction makes you appreciate that there is more skill to it than Hollywood was ever able to convey.

The feedlots here stagger the imagination. They are known as CAFOs now. That is the official, politically correct, term for "confined-animal feeding operations." Perhaps 100,000 or more cows are confined in a very small space. For those of you unfamiliar with the term, they call them feedlots because that is what they are. Range cattle are brought there to eat a great deal under controlled conditions and then sent off to be food. It is not a sight for the faint of heart or those who have well developed olfactory senses. There are perhaps ten "CAFO's" in the space of a few miles. It is a sight better left in the backcountry. Feedlots are like chicken houses, those massive ones that serve the purpose of either gathering eggs or fattening the poultry. I didn't really lose my appetite after seeing these things, but I probably could have if I had dwelled on it. I am sure I will not want steak tonight.

The Mountain Time Zone and the Texas state line arrived at Muleshoe. Less than 5,000 people call it home. So does The National Mule Memorial, the "unsung beast of burden" to be remembered for its place in history. Interesting. It may be the only monument to an animal that cannot reproduce itself, is not yet close to extinction, and yet is called a "Memorial." It was erected in 1965 after a fund raising effort that actually brought a 21-cent donation from a farmer in Russia and they are proud of it. It is a statue of a mule down near the grain elevator. It is larger than life and the local literature describes it as an "ideal picture taking opportunity."

There are mules here; they have a rodeo of mules in September. I was sorry I missed that and the other "mule related activities", whatever that may mean. Bird watchers come here too since the sand hill crane winters here. There may be more here at that time than anywhere else in the United States. Prairie dogs are a big deal here too. It is, for all of this, just another road junction, of U.S. 70 and U.S. 84. Either one will get you out of this town of rodeo signs and cattle car sidings that will move the beef to market. It is not a pretty place. People do not stay here because of the aesthetics of the main street, or because they want to be close to the "World's Largest Muleshoe" housed up near the old railroad station. It is not a place one would imagine enjoying a vacation, or even a cold winter night. The people who live here do so for the work or because they were born here and have responsibilities. There even may be a few who enjoy its ambiance. Muleshoe just isn't all that attractive to me.

The trip to Canyon, where the Palo Duro Canyon State Park is located is short if confusing for lack of landmarks and decent directions. The State of Texas has some lovely Parks. It is hard to believe that this canyon is here from even a mile or two away. You drive the very flat prairie almost to the gate before beginning a descent into what does look like the Grand Canyon. The locals say it was carved from a tributary of the Red River and it was a Comanche stronghold for a very long time. Apparently, one Col. Ronald S. Mackenzie and a part of the 4th Cavalry were wandering across these plains back in 1874 and found a remarkable number of Indians who had taken refuge here. They were "menacing" the area, we are told, so the Colonel merely captured their horses and burned their villages. After this act of "compassion", the Comanche were forced to walk back to their "prison-like" reservations in Oklahoma and spend the rest of their days in captivity. The literature of the Park recounts this in a remarkably matter of fact way.

Aside from all that gruesome history, it is an interesting place. Some of the canyon walls are 1,000 feet high. The erosion from the river must have begun long before the Red River had a name. I remark to a local that you sort of expect to see John Wayne or another of the "cowboy heroes" hustling up the trail with an Indian war party right behind them. I am told, had I been here a number of years ago, I could have seen just that. Many movies were made here and it is a real treasure well hidden. Putting the lie to the fact that this is but rural culture, there is a great outdoor amphitheater here where plays are presented from late June until August. The most likely one to be seen is called "Texas, A Musical Drama." In the style of this part of the world, bar-b-cue is included in the price of admission, and the handbills assure "ya'll come, even if you are non-theater goers!"

Once I had settled into the campsite after arriving early Saturday, I rewarded myself with a nap while it was still shady in my corner of this stark yet lovely place. The campsites were varied in vegetation and type.

I was in one nearer the top of the canyon that had perhaps 60 spaces in it with a few trees and hard packed clay.

I went wandering for some exercise and scenery. I soon was exchanging "howdy's" with most everyone and found that the majority of my neighbors were Shriners, here for a potluck dinner that night which was why there was a big tent in the middle of the "cul-de-sac". A couple of the campers had noticed the California license plates and after satisfying their curiosity that I was indeed from there, I was invited to join them for dinner. It was not a natural choice for me, but when "Jimmy Love" and "Hooter" (accompanied by his English bulldog "Happy"), invite you to dinner in the Texas panhandle, you say simply, "why, thank you sir." They were such polite people, it seemed the right thing to do. When the time to eat arrived, Jimmy came to get me. I was introduced to the "women folk" and "set a spell" while eating some of the best smoked ham, country sausage and pumpkin pecan cobbler I ever had. The people I met seem fascinated by my trip. Their disbelief that I am actually doing this alone puzzles me but many think I am somewhere between Lewis and Clark for even trying. If I heard one more "Well isn't that wonderful!" I might have given back some of the sausage.

They are sincere and wonderful people who welcome strangers without reservation. I was happy I had overcome my initial reluctance, even if Happy and Hooter and Jimmy were part of the reason. It was quite a feast and the people were as interesting and varied as the food.

On the way back to the van, I realized that the wind is with me now as it always is on the prairie. I mentioned it to Jimmie, who remarked, "If you don't feel wind after dawn, you have likely left the Panhandle." It blows down from the Rocky Mountains with nothing in its way. It brings coolness to a hot day, but stings the eyes and a never-ending murmur accompanies all that you do. It bothers some to the point of distraction and insanity. But if you live in or visit the Panhandle, it will be there, waiting. It is annoying at first, but it disappears from my consciousness, like the sound of traffic or a train at night. I am sure it will be with me until the southern humidity takes its place.

The day of rest on Sunday is pleasant. The weather is holding although it may not for long. With luck, I will get this next leg—one of the longest on this section of the journey—done. If not, I won't. I will figure that out tomorrow.

-2-

The departure was bittersweet. I was anxious to continue the adventure, but sorry to leave the people and the place. It was a quiet campsite by Sunday night as the Shriners and other locals packed up to leave by noon. I met Patsy and Austin, part of the campground "host" program at dusk the night before I left.

Those of you unfamiliar with this type of travel should know that "hosts" appear in the state parks and usually are located at the first space near the "front" of the campsite area. There may be more than one as here, since there are a number of camping areas. Usually they are a husband and wife who volunteer to bring their trailer and sit a week and answer questions so the state employees can deal with real emergencies. They get free rent, usually love to talk, and can be great company early in the season when there are not many others on the grounds. They remind me of congenial Bed and Breakfast owners who enjoy the company of strangers and do not tire easily of the same questions asked over and over.

It was threatening rain and I had decided to go on my internal generator and internal water for the night since I didn't want to get out and slide around until my wheelchair stuck in the mud in the early morning. Amarillo is a word, from an Indian dialect, for yellow soil. I was sure, if wet, it would be a slippery as ice.

I first met Austin and Patti when they came by to tell me I was right to get unhooked since there was "some weather" in the area and they had been told to warn those few of us still here about it. "Some weather" to these folks means a tornado or a particularly vicious thunderstorm. If it got real bad, they said, I should get to the stone building where the showers were. The clay was not going to make that easy so I decided I would drive as far over there until I found a cement walk, put the ramp down on it, and head indoors if the weather came. Thankfully, it passed to the north of us. It was not something I was looking forward to dealing with in the middle of the night.

In the morning I stopped to say goodbye to my hosts. They shared their coffee with me and we talked a bit. Austin gave me a route to Tulsa that would avoid Oklahoma City altogether and get me off Interstate 40 sooner than I had hoped. We said goodbye in the early coolness of the now near empty canyon. For some reason, I was sorry to leave this place. Perhaps I was beginning to unwind and learn that the trip was not about time, but people and places.

FOUR

SHAMROCK TEXAS, OKLAHOMA CITY AND KEYSTONE STATE PARK

After my reluctant goodbyes, it was on to I-40, which may be the heaviest traveled cross-country route in the United States. It is U.S. 66 reincarnated as a limited access 70 mile an hour, bone jarring strip of four, six and at times, eight lanes of concrete. The seams in the road bounce you up and down enough that you are sure teeth will soon begin to leave your head, especially in the more heavily traveled right lane. If anything is going to come loose in the van and fly through the air, it will be on this highway. Maintaining the road under the traffic and weather conditions it endures is nearly impossible. From Illinois to California, it carries millions of tons of commerce, thousands of people on vacations and travelers who need to cross the country by car, and of course now and then the odd man in a van looking for a novel experience. It is a mighty superhighway that passes through or near cities and towns from the old song about Route 66. In that way it is impressive, but it is not interesting.

Shamrock, Texas got the nod for breakfast and fuel. It was not because of its name or inherent beauty. The town was not immediately evident, but that is what the exit sign said. It was a convenient stop and I was hungry and the van was thirsty. There was an incessant drizzle by now and the only thing that made this exit more desirable was that I could see the restaurant and fuel station from the Interstate.

When I parked and tried to open the doors to the van, there were no more thoughts of breakfast. As I pressed the remote control, to open the side doors and deploy the ramp, the silence was deafening. I suddenly had the sinking realization that there was no electric power to either open the doors or lower the lift. This is not a minor annoyance, since it is the only orderly way for me to get out. The other option is to jump or fall out the driver's door from a height of about five feet. That is not a preferred method of egress. Trouble was, at this point there was not a good way to tell anyone in the gas and diesel section, which is of course self-serve, that I had a problem and what they might be able to do about it. It could be very simple, since the switch had worked earlier in the day it seemed its abrupt stop might indicate a short or something else a " shade tree" mechanic might be able to figure out. Unlike the days when Route 66 was the road traveled, all the "service" stations anywhere near most Interstate highways are more grocery store than service. You get to pump your own gas and pay some 17 year old who is more responsible for food stocking than he is for the fuel. This appears to be another attempt to make us believe that cars are infallible when it really means they have become so complicated that a roadside gas station might change your battery, but it would take them all day to get to and change the spark plugs. We like to believe that we buy a car and merely service it every 15,000 miles and it will run. It doesn't breakdown. Traveling solo in something as complicated as a van with electric doors and a lift is, in some ways, an act of faith that all this is true. There are simply no alternatives. I always feel a certain loss of control while using the lift. It requires many moving parts and while suspended above the earth a certain act of trust is required just as it is when using the Landing Signal Lights on an aircraft carrier at night. The lift is only powered by the truck's engine battery and there is no way to switch to the larger, so-called "house" batteries in the rear. I pondered awhile, since there was little else to do in the drizzle that made the waves of fuel and breakfast seekers move even faster around me. The lift can be lowered by electrical override switch or manually, but not alone. It is at least a two person operation. I wondered if Shamrock had a sheriff's sub-station. I thought about, and rejected the idea of dialing 911. It occurred to me that I really had no idea why the lift would not work. I tried the emergency override switches, which did nothing. If it were lowered manually, that would get me out, but would not fix what might be a complicated problem.

Thanks to cellular technology, I spoke with the Service Manager for Leisure Travel Van in Canada, who gave me the name of a lift installer in Oklahoma City. He strongly advised going there before doing anything else. I now faced a few hours in the van with whatever was in the refrigerator until I could reach him in downtown Oklahoma City. That seemed a reasonable solution to the first problem. Problem two was that I did not have enough fuel for the trip. After three tries, I flagged down a reasonably friendly soul who agreed to pump gas for me and his friend took my money inside to pay for it. This second part of the transaction was another act of faith since I did not know either of them and they both looked sleepy, rumpled and in need of a shave. They were, it turns out, hauling a trailer behind their car across country from Visalia California. Another random act of kindness by strangers appeared to have helped save me from faulty technology.

That brought an end to any hope for side trips to Enid on this drizzly day. It even brought an end to stops, for that matter, as I sped along the Interstate to downtown Oklahoma City. The trip was about three hours and took away whatever scenery might have been had on the route my latest best friend Austin had suggested.

A friendly, if gruff man, who owned the lift repair business, identified the problem. A wire had been left hanging loose; either due to some repair work I had done before I left or had been so since the van was equipped with the lift. It had come in contact with the exhaust and had burned halfway through. Fortunately, the circuit breaker installed in case something stupid like that happens worked. Only the power to the lift and door was interrupted. Had it not worked, the whole van might have "fried" as he put it, and I would have learned what it was like to exit the driver's seat through the door from five feet up. He explained all this to me in exquisite detail while I sat there in the driveway of his establishment. He knew his business, and had it fixed in under an hour. The rain persisted in spurts through it all. The only question that remained was how far I would get before nightfall. The owner gave me very good directions to quickly exit the city and go on to the northeast. I decided to drive on to see how far I would get. The "shortcut" put me on the first toll road of the trip. I had forgotten what a privilege it is to pay to drive a road through the middle of nowhere.

Oklahoma has some of the best road sign directions I have seen so far, and since I didn't get lost at the end of the day as I had a habit of doing, I made my original destination, Keystone State Park, outside of Tulsa at about 6:30 PM. It was clear, cool, and green. My campsite was on a lake and quite beautiful. I would have stayed a few days longer, but the next night they were full. A religious group had booked every site capable of electricity and water. I had dinner outside as the sun dropped into the trees beyond the lake and I was able to chat with a most amiable neighbor who stopped to say hello and look over the van. He was a fisherman with a trailer, a pontoon boat and a vast array of fishing gear. He seemed interesting and he and I both professed regret that I would only be there that night. He said I seemed like someone with whom he would like to talk. I took it as a compliment. As darkness came so did a cool breeze, and after bidding him a nice life, I reluctantly moved indoors. It was almost heaven, and a great end to a long and intense day. Another obstacle had been overcome, and another day was in the logbook. Somehow these victories over adversity not of my own making, which I figure out how to overcome, raise my mood. It is almost as if subconsciously I am proving that once again, it can be done. In this mood, sleep comes quickly, since all seems right with the world.

FIVE

A TOWN IN OKLAHOMA, A TOWN IN TWO STATES, PARIS, AND A PLACE CALLED HOPE

U.S. Routes and State Roads passing through little towns made up my day. I spent only 40 miles on the Interstate Highway. I am delighted. The ones I travel are the kind that makes believers of the out-of-state people who do not think that the "Reduce Speed Ahead " sign means them, or that you had better start slowing down now. This is "Smokey and the Bandit" country, for those of you who remember the personage of Buford T. Justice, the Sheriff with the slow witted son chasing a truckload of beer from Louisiana to Georgia in the movie of the same name.

The scenery is quite lovely. The green is brilliant on the rolling hills through the middle of the country. Those of us who have "done time" on the Left and Right coasts tend to forget that it is beautiful here. It is also not crowded and for the most part the people are unpretentious—except about religion and high school football. In towns like McAlester and Hugo and Atoka, there are stadiums that seat 20,000 in towns all of much lesser populations. The heartbeat is the children, sports, and church. It seems no one who lives in these places ever stops caring about those.

I spent a long morning in a small town in Oklahoma. The population is still under 10,000 and I guess it is a suburb of Tulsa, in the Oklahoma sense of that word. It is about forty miles away and is not yet a "bedroom town" for the big city and has some industry. The town is along the Arkansas River, and was founded as an agricultural society as were most here. It now is supported by truck farming, livestock products, and some newer industry. It was settled by a large group of Bulgarians who emigrated here in the 1920's looking for fertile ground and freedom and found both.

This was a substitute for my side trip to Enid. I apologize to whomever I promised a trip to that place. This is different. Enid is bigger I am told and not nearly as curious as this small town. I sat in a coffee shop of the old style on the Main Street and listened to the conversation of the place that gives you the rhythm of life in a town of this size. I watched the town go to work on this May morning. They looked as harried and as sleepy as people anywhere. In the coffee shop and on the street, some were dressed in the "old" style, and the simply old who wore straw cowboy hats and jeans and a T-shirt with a name of a farm product on it. New Balance cross trainer shoes seemed to be the footwear of choice, at least for the trip to town. Not many wore boots. Some of these folks looked like they were up long before the sun doing whatever one does for or to livestock at that hour. Others were the "new" crowd, not necessarily younger, but the "yuppies" of small town America. They drove a mini-van or SUV and some had likely just dropped kids at day care. They looked bleary eyed as they hustled through the McDonald's drive thru lane across the street. They get L.L. Bean and Land's End catalogues here, too, so they look as if they could be in any part of your town—or even you.

I wandered down the street to the Post Office after some conversation and my fill of coffee and eavesdropping on the locals. I am aware that note has been taken of my license plate by now. The conversation in the Post Office as I mailed off some pictures to be posted on the website was about the current state of the main street, which was, to be kind, so dug up it looked like some mortar rounds had been lobbed onto it. My interest in all this got me directions to where I could find the Mayor, who had a real life as a Pharmacist. We talked of the town and its "progress", the state government and its influence here as well as the federal one at Washington. He didn't have much use for either from the way he talked about them. I asked where the funds have come from to pave the street, since it was clear it was not from just the hard earned dollars of the town's citizens. He allowed that help from the entities he had been reviling had been needed, and he admitted that the local Congressman and the State Senator from this area had helped a good deal. He supposed they really weren't bad fellows, they seemed to care, but he just wasn't sure about the rest of them, from other parts of the state or the country. They seemed to be a lot of them who were more interested in their own problems and taking pleasure at public expense than in the good of the whole state or the country. Obviously, this was not a liberal democrat, or a tolerant libertarian that I was spending the morning with, but he was genuinely interested in the welfare of his town, which seemed to me what mattered, not what he thought of the peccadilloes of the officials in Washington.

It was his hope (and mine for those who drive it) that at least the gravel base would be put down this week before it rains. He told me of the merchants' concern for business amongst all the orange cones and detours. In an almost reverent way, he showed me the plans for the pedestrian mall, and how the storefronts will look as if in an earlier time. He was proud of his town and "his" people and glad that he could help bring life back to the downtown Main Street and that the businesses would not all leave it for the highway and the inevitable strip malls. This is something of an antique capital of the county, or perhaps more and he clearly didn't want to see all that business end up outside the town jurisdiction five miles away on the highway. Some had already begun that migration. I did not question the purity of his motives, but business taxation was clearly an issue the town elders had thought about.

We talked of other improvements that were planned. He stressed that he hoped to keep the town as it was, but admitted that the new turnpike and the improvements made to keep the town from flooding would put pressure on it to become a "bedroom" town for Tulsa as time went on. He didn't seem to grasp how difficult it would be to keep the town "values" when that happened. He spoke as if dreaming; as I have heard others speak so often of the way it would be when inevitable expansion took place. Even the industry that has moved there recently has caused whole new neighborhoods to be built. He saw that as good for the town, but had no answer when asked what it would be like if three times that number of people moved in to town and needed schools for their kids. Surely, downtown could remain charming, but just as the antique businesses had led to mall building, could K-Mart be far behind? He seemed to hope not, but didn't seem like he had thought much about it either. Standing on the corner of Main Street and Elm, it was easy to forget the town beyond, to retreat into the small town mindset, but would it still be that way five years from now when there were five times the police and fire needs? He said he didn't know, but he sure hoped it wouldn't be all that bad.

He answered many more questions about the town, its history and its' people, who, as he put it "care about their neighbors". I am still having trouble understanding small towns, particularly ones like this that may soon become big because they are inviting it to happen. I worry that it is happening because the Chamber of Commerce thinks it a good idea despite what most of the people who live there may think. They are being told that this will bring progress and that will bring a better quality of life. Well maybe it will. But it will mean huge capital and salary outlays they have not even thought about, and failure to police properly and prepare the children for it all will bring crime and drugs and poverty and all other urban ills. Will that be a better quality of life? Have they even thought about whether the quality they have now is worth preserving? I am conflicted by these islands with only tenuous connections to larger places. Is this the good life, or merely a small place filled with small minds, prejudice and pictures of grandmother on the mantel? I do not know. I do not judge them harshly because of the way they see it. They like it this way and that is fine. I am just not sure they are going to like becoming more like Tulsa when the time will come when it does.

I asked of the industry and the lives of the children. He answered pleasantly enough but I left with the sense that there was more to this place than he had told me. On this lovely spring morning, however, I decided there was more to see and do. I left the conversation not knowing whether I had just spoken to George F. Babbit's great grandson or a true visionary. I went to look at the schools and the children of such a town. As I did, he told me to be sure to blow the horn just past the gasoline station at the edge of town as I left since he would to be home for lunch and lived in the house across the street. He said I might see him and his Dad and his son engaged in a wiffle ball tournament they had started last spring.

The children here all seem to want to be at least partially blond this spring, and most are. They seem no different, if perhaps less threatened, than your own. The people of the town clearly make a special place for them. These children were the ones I had heard spoken about by the farmers and construction workers in the booths in the coffee shop earlier that day. They talked of them as if they were all related. It actually took some serious eavesdropping to assure myself that they were not. The Wilson boy who was such a good student and the Burleson kid, who without a doubt was the best football player to come out of that part of the world since Troy Aikman graduated from a school just down the road.

I left much sooner than I would have liked, but I thought I understood the place a little better than when I came. I saw the Mayor and his son as I drove out. The boy may have been five or six, but he was clearly having the most fun. Grandpa was pitching and the Mayor was running the ball down, but mostly spending his lunch hour making his child laugh. I blew the horn and they all waved as if a good friend were leaving, instead of a curious guy from California who asked a lot of questions. I was grateful for that.

I spent the rest of the day rolling through other small towns. I thought of how all our lives would be enriched if we could be concerned with the social good of a town, and take the time at lunch to make a child laugh.

Along the route I was traveling, many of the main streets had been abandoned for the strip malls along the highway. It made me think that perhaps "Hizzonor" was right. Even if the place turns out to be a little bit glitzy for some, it is better to save it than to let it go, even if the highway becomes the real center of commerce. It need not become the substitute for Main Street as it had in so many of these places.

-2-

I did make a side trip to Paris (Texas, that is) and Archer. A billboard will tell you that it is the biggest Paris on this side of the Atlantic. I am sure that is funny to someone. It is a dusty Texas city. There is a lovely restored Victorian Mansion built by a Confederated General named Sam Maxey. His family actually lived in the house until about forty years ago. He was one of those many West Pointers like Robert E. Lee, caught between his allegiance to the Army and his home. Maxey choose Texas.

Frank James, brother of Jesse spent his retirement here clerking in a Dry Goods store. Belle Starr, who sounds more like a stripper than the "outlaw queen" ran a farm nearby. There are about 26,000 souls there now, none as infamous as these, but the visitor's bureau is willing to tell you all about these infamous characters of the past. Archer, with its 1,900 residents, looks a little like the town from "The Last Picture Show." It almost gives you the feeling of being in black and white like the movie. It is small and once was a retail and shipping center, but now has a few shallow oil wells to keep it together and it is the county seat of Archer County. I never did see the theater, but that may have been my fault since I was pressing on by that time. Archer shows no sign that it was the site of the filming, although I read in a local paper there has been a fuss about whether it was really done there or not. There apparently has always been some controversy here about just how much of it was. Some claim it was in a town nearby. I suppose it possible that somewhere, Peter Bogdonavich and Cybil Shepard made a wrong turn. I guess it is also possible that Hollywood might not have told the whole truth. I doubt that would surprise many.

-3-

Texarkana, the town of two states, is a unique place. It is referred to as the twin cities, and for good reason. It is divided, yet united. The main street is called State Line Avenue. It is in fact, exactly that, the state line between Texas and Arkansas. Right down the white line. Even the local citizens occasionally get disoriented, but most of the time it is largely ignored.

Who named the place, or decided it should be built there, and why it has the state line running through it has never completely been resolved. The most popular and accepted version credits a railroad surveyor named Gus Knobel. He actually thought he was at the junction of Texas, Arkansas and Louisiana that is how the "na" got stuck on the end of the name. Why Gus would want to found and put the name of a town on the corner of three states is never adequately explained, but I can only suppose he never imagined the kind of chaos that might cause or had a very strange sense of humor.

The motto of the town is "Twice As Nice." The "twice" part is certainly true since it has two city governments, police departments and fire departments. There are some very pretty things here. The State Line Post Office for one is architecturally interesting. As would be expected, since half of it is in each state, there are different zip codes. The Federal Building also has a plaza in front where you can stand in both states at once.

Scott Joplin, the jazz pianist and composer was born here. He was pretty much the King of Ragtime. He composed the tune, the "Entertainer", later made more famous as the theme of the movie " The Sting" in 1973. It in turn stirred a revival in Ragtime in the 1970's and Joplin was awarded a Pulitzer posthumously in 1976 likely as a result of the renewed interest.

There is a Bi-State Justice Center, which is like none other. The county, state and law enforcement agencies of the two states share it. There was a piece of elaborate legislation passed so that the legal jurisdiction of each state does not apply inside the building. Thus, a Texas Judge may hear a case in a courtroom that is technically in Arkansas, but it doesn't violate jurisdictional lines.

The monuments and memorials and historical markers along State Line Avenue give some idea of the rich and diverse history of this place. Jim Bowie passed through here to his way to defend the Alamo in 1836. He went through here in 1819 so it must have been a long walk. Hernando De Soto was here in 1541 and he hung a mutineer from a nearby tree. For some reason, wherever this is mentioned, it is made clear that it was in Texas. The Daughters of the American Revolution erected a plaque there in 1926. There is a monument to the Confederate Soldiers, erected in 1918 and one to Korean and Vietnam dead from across four states erected in 1988 when few remembered there was a Korean War and few monuments to the Vietnam dead were being planned. They are only two blocks apart, and are quite complimentary.

These all belie the tension that can come from the boosters from one side of the street or the other. The people seem to enjoy their unique status. The number of "what ifs" that one could construct for a town like this are enormous, but, over the years, they seem to have thought of most of them. It is not clear how much enmity there is on each side of State Line Avenue. The potential is certainly there, but these people smile a lot and are amused by visitors' questions. The store names usually include the town and state, as in "Miller's Dry Goods, Texarkana, Texas" and "The Bakery Shop, Texarkana, Arkansas". My visit was a pleasant surprise, and longer than I had thought it would be. The people were unfailingly pleasant and did not find it odd that they "shared" a state line or a unique culture and surely saw no reason to do anything about it to make their lives less complicated.

Peaceful sleep came at Millwood State Park in Ashdown, AK nearby. It was in a pine forest gravely injured by the ice storms of the past winter, as was much of the area near here. The pine trees along the route and here in the park lost most of their lower branches. The Ranger tells me that it will take all year to just try to clear them off the trees and pick them up. There is a heightened fire danger in the whole state. This is an old park. I suspect most of the folks I saw in the ten hours there were more interested in how the catfish and bass were biting in the mosquito producing waters nearby than by the state of the loblolly pines or the stately grandeur of the Canadian geese that strutted through the place. With a new fishing season, these folks had come out to take advantage of that. They seemed less friendly and only slyly curious about my license plates and me. I got an occasional wave on my evening stroll to the lake, but I equaled it in stares. The fellow about two campsites over, who appeared to be there with his entire extended family of some 15 people and more vehicles and boat trailers than they could use, spent the better part of the first half hour I was there just staring at me and the van. Any attempt to be friendly was simply ignored. He just stared. I thought he had lost the ability to speak, but that was later disproved by a shouted discussion he had with what appeared to be a daughter. It was the first time I could remember a lack of geniality in a campsite. Perhaps the fishing was more important than conversation. This was clearly home to the geese, but only a place to park for the night for some of us.

-4-

The rising sun found me on the road to Hope, Arkansas. I wanted to see the town ever since the Democratic Convention in 1992 when the now former, then soon to be, President William Jefferson Clinton was shown sitting in front of the sign on the railroad station. I was not planning on much of a pilgrimage to the town where the President spent his very early years, I just wanted to see that sign on the station. The town did not disappoint me. It was as shabby as I expected it to be. It is clear that very little has been made yet of the fact that one of our Presidents was born and lived his early years there. The house he was born in is there, but has not been owned by a Clinton for 30 years. He actually only lived here with his maternal grandparents for his first four years, where it is noted, he learned to "walk, talk, laugh, read, and pray." The station looks spiffy and the main street looks like any other quaint Arkansas town. It is the side streets of these places that always amaze. Even now, these many years after he has left, the town remains what is known politely in the south as a "trailer town." It was hard to imagine a boy on the street dreaming of going to Harvard or to Oxford University much less becoming the President of the United States. It seems far more likely he would marry a distant cousin from a town down the road, raise his kids, and work until he dropped dead at fifty-five, overweight from greasy food, smoking too much, drinking too much beer and watching too many football games, while known only to his family and friends. A place called Hope is just that, a place, not a magic kingdom.

SIX

"SWINGING BRIDGE", JACKSON, MISSISSIPPI

I have reached another welcome two-day stop. The weather is wonderful and the traveling along U.S. 82 and 167 was pleasant and uncluttered. The country was Arkansan, Texan, Cajun, and now Mississippian. Towns named El Dorado, Stamps, Magnolia, Homer, Bernice, Plain Dealing, Bayou Chanute, and Clinton. Whole cultures passed in a drive through Arkansas, Texas, Louisiana, and across the Mississippi into Alabama and the heart of Dixie. I crossed the Mississippi at Vicksburg after a brief drive on I-20. This would not be my last encounter with the mighty river, but it was the first of the trip. I had seen the Red River and the Pecos and the Rio Grande. It felt a bit like a bird watcher who is adding to a life list of rivers I have now seen that I had only read about or heard in song.

There is nothing tangible here at the campsite that I would recommend as a place to stay other than a quiet pine grove. The advertisements about a shopping center chock full of discount stores and other amenities are, at least this year, a shell of what was advertised, and a gleam in the eye of the owner. The "Swinging Bridge" tastefully adorning all the literature was actually about a mile and a half from the park and was in no way connected to it or its' owner. I saw it when I left only because it was on a shortcut I wanted to take; otherwise I would have missed it entirely. Cable TV and e-mail access at the sites also are a belief rather than a reality, although it was made very clear that "several" sites had them. Mine just wasn't one of them. Two were so equipped it appeared, so it was not a false advertisement, but it pushed the truth toward allegation. There is shade, however, and for Mississippi this time of year, weather that is quite lovely. None of those things are of the owner's making, of course, but it is well back from the road and there are no trains involved. Trains and campgrounds are inexorably linked. I do not know why, but where you find one you will likely find the other.

Jackson is in a rural part of the state. But then most of Mississippi is essentially rural when seen through the eyes of someone like me. It was founded in 1821 as a trading post for furs and other things headed down river to New Orleans. What recommended it as a place to live at all was that it was on a high bluff along the river. Founded by a French trader, it originally was LeFleur's Bluff. Later, the state wanted to move the capital from the Natchez area, because of its atrocious climate and its location, as opposed to Jackson's merely hot and humid climate and more central location. After some surveying around the area, the Lattimore brothers found the bluff after following the Pearl River south and west. They are alleged to have reported back to the Assembly, which had commissioned them, that this was an area of healthful climate, abundant timber, and navigable waters, which was close to the then very important Natchez Trail. Apparently this was enough to make believers out of the boys in the Assembly and in 1821 (November actually and the 28th to be exact about it) voted to move the seat of the central government to the site and to name it in honor of Major General Andrew Jackson, who had come through the place after the Battle of New Orleans which was as a result of the War of 1812. I say as a result because the battle, in which he decidedly thrashed the British, was actually fought after England had sued for peace and the war was over. There was no CNN or e-mail in those days. He was far from Washington and until riders reached him he could not know they had surrendered. The British commander obviously was suffering from the same illusion. Jackson later did a rather important and seminal turn as President of the United States. So it was *Au Revior Monsieur Lefleur*, and hello to the "city" of Jackson from that day forth. The Assembly appropriated the munificent sum of $3,200 to build a state house, awarded the contract and got a thirty foot square, two story brick building.

The importance of the Natchez Trail, originally known as a "Trace" and its place in history and in placing the new capital cannot be understated. It was the main thoroughfare of the old "southwest." It extended nearly 450 miles from Nashville Tennessee to Natchez Mississippi. It began as a Native American footpath and was used heavily by the early settlers (including General Jackson). Post riders and boatman too, used it regularly. Farmers would build flat bottom boats to ride the current down river to markets well beyond their reach otherwise and then sell everything including the lumber from the boats and walk home, sometimes a hundred miles or more. It seems nearly inconceivable now that this would be a profitable way to move goods to market, but it was and they had lots of time. They needed to be home for spring planting, otherwise, time didn't much matter. It was a very busy place. Merewether Lewis, who at the time was the Governor of the Louisiana Territories, but of Lewis and Clarke Expedition fame died while on the Trace while on his way to Washington D. C. Depending on which scholar you choose to believe, he was either murdered at a place called Grinder's Stand, or committed suicide during a raging fever due to his neurosyphilis, which he and many of the men had contracted from the Native Americans they came in contact with during his epic trek through the now western United States.

There has been an attempt to restore the old Trace route, which is only about 15% complete. There are so many roads that cross it or follow it, it will never be a foot trail like the Appalachian, but there is a Parkway, much like the Blue Ridge that follows much of the old route. Had I been paying attention, and not still been in my "scheduled stop mode" this would have been an excellent addition to my trip. As it was, I saw only a small part of it. To hike it, one would have to walk the roads since it is estimated that only 7% remains unpaved and protected by the National Park Service. The evidence of its early heavy use includes places near the end where grooves 12 feet deep are found. The thousands of feet that trod it made them in the red clay soil.

Mississippi adopted the Constitution in 1832 and that assured that the capital would have a reason to exist at all and they then built more capacious quarters. In 1961, after having survived a reasonably checkered career as offices and several threats to burn it down, the capital became a museum and is a lovely old place more Greek than southern. The Governor's Mansion built at about the same time has had quite a different fate. It became the seat of municipal government for the City of Jackson. It was built for $8,000 and 140 years later still serves the same purpose. There are no better deals in real estate than that.

General Sherman came through here three times although the local literature never made it clear why it took him twice as long to ravage the capital of this small rural place than it did for him to burn down most of Atlanta. There are many such anomalies about the "War between the States" as it is known hereabouts (there was nothing, southerners will tell you, "civil" in any meaning of that word about that war) which can be vague or have many explanations. The locals profess not to know why he didn't burn down the government buildings, or are at least unclear about it. There may have been a Masonic Lodge in one of them, or a church, or something else he respected is how one story goes. The fact that they may have been temporary hospitals sounds more likely it to me.

Jackson housed some 8,000 souls in 1900 and in 1990 had more than 395,000. Now a metropolis by some standards with teaching hospitals, a college, "two regional Malls", whatever that odious term may mean, and commerce mostly as a "distribution center." Or that is what the Chamber of Commerce calls it. I think, in English, it means that lots of trucks, buses, boats and planes move things through here to Dallas to the west and Atlanta to the east. It is a pleasant place, taken altogether, unless it is July or August at about five o'clock and the sun is still high and all you have is lemonade and a swamp cooler to get you through the night.

-2-

In the peaceful shade of the pine trees, far back from the highway at Swinging Bridge, I enjoyed an extraordinary series of conversations with a man named Buddy. He is a legend here, mainly because he pulled in one day last November and hasn't yet decided to leave, but never pays another month's rent until the very last day. "Boots" is his dog of eight months who has had at least two serious operations since Buddy got him as a pup. When he bought him, he became sick almost immediately and the veterinarian suggested he take the dog back. Buddy thought that was a little like giving a sick child back to the hospital. He also is convinced the breeder would merely have disposed of the six week old pup. So he kept him and paid for the expensive surgeries that allow him to breathe almost normally. That is why Buddy is still here, nurturing his dog and friend Boots back to health. The fact that Boots lived through the extraordinary pulmonary surgeries is a testament to his spirit as well. Maybe that is why they are so close. No one stops here for more than 24 hours without having an opportunity to meet the pair. No one refers to one without the other since they are inseparable.

Buddy retired at 53 as a civilian employee of the Navy after 33 years of federal service, including two tours with the Army in Vietnam. He appears to be as happy and as smart a man as I have met. Originally from Meridian Mississippi, he started traveling in a van the size of mine about 10 years ago. He liked it and kept buying bigger ones. He now has a 35-foot motor coach. He lives there with Boots and thinks and reads a great deal. He listens to the radio from time to time, reads a newspaper and prefers the history channel if television is in his plans for the day. He sits in a chair outside the coach door and plays with Boots and thinks about the meaning of life, as he has known it. He has a limitless curiosity about people and places and is a wonderful storyteller once he gets over his shyness with strangers.

He left school in the third grade, enlisted in the Army at 20. After nine years, having long before figured out that stripes on your sleeve were equal to money in your pocket, he had his high school diploma (GED) and was a Sergeant. He decided to leave the Army since he was due to re-enlist one month short of finishing his second tour in Vietnam. He knew the consequences of reenlistment in those days were 30 days combat leave and a return trip to that Southeast Asian paradise for 365 more days. So he decided it was a good time to go. He applied for an apprenticeship program, and by the time the Navy sent him on his way he had become a master metal worker on aircraft carriers and nuclear submarines at the Norfolk, Virginia shipyard. He can't think of a reason to regret leaving and has an insight into things that is simple, direct, and logical. He is not the smartest man in the world but I would put him in a room with any number of the members of the current Chattering Class in the world press and he would get along just fine. He is as devoted to his southern roots as he is to Boots. There are folks at Harvard and Yale and Stanford that could not carry his books. His patience in most things appears to be infinite. He does not wear his beliefs on his sleeve, but he will talk about and defend them with passion. He is a loyal and patriotic American citizen who, as near as I can tell has no racist tendencies at all. He voted last year to leave the confederate Stars and Bars as part of the flag of the state of Mississippi. He will tell you, when you ask, that in a democratic society, that a vote is the will of the people, and therefore this was the will of a majority of the people, that it has nothing to do with the south's segregationist past and he is proud enough of it that he will give you a pin with the flag on it should you agree that you aren't just going to throw it away when you leave.

I had remarked as to how dense and angry the campground "security guard" seemed to be. He "patrolled" the complex every once in awhile and seemed to want to be friendly, but didn't really know how to be and usually left seeming to be upset. Buddy spoke in a soft voice for a long time about it, taking great pains to explain why he acts like he does. He told me that the fellow was a typical rural Mississippi boy, a lot like himself when he was young, who had quit school as is too common there to "do other things ", take care of a family, run the streets, work a farm, or because school just didn't seem relevant. He said that he had the same chances to do what he, Buddy, had done if he would take advantage of the opportunity. It would be very hard, Buddy admitted. He had found it very hard to compete with others while trying to make up the deficit and the feelings of inferiority while he caught up with his peers. Buddy had been stubborn and curious enough, and in my view, intelligent enough, to know that leaving school when he did was not the correct decision. What our friend the guard needed to understand, Buddy pointed out, was that he had made the wrong decision, but that it was all right and there was still a chance, despite the time it would take, a long and humbling time to be sure, to make up for it.

These and other rural southern truths are things that Buddy under-stands and can talk about with great wisdom. He knows why the south-ern white male is dirt poor in many cases. They tossed their chance at education and advancement the minute they could so that they could hunt and fish and, in some cases, help Daddy run the farm. Southern males identify strongly with their fathers as heroes. They likely did the same thing, so the circle is perpetuated. They did it because they thought it right and had received very little counsel or guidance from their fami-lies or substandard teachers in inferior public schools who were over-whelmed by the sheer numbers who required their attention. Our friend and so many others like him never got any help thinking through the consequence of that decision. Buddy says he never got any help either. They are the "Kleenex' of southern society, tossed away to fend for themselves. They become angry and develop a sense of righteousness far exceeding their capabilities. They thought at the time that was the right thing to do, but as Buddy points out, there are not many 10 year old kids that know the right thing to do. However, the same kid does know, maybe five, or ten years later. But rather than go out and try do better as hard as that may be, they accept the earlier decision because of a false pride or belief that they couldn't make a mistake and never really are at peace with themselves. They remain angry. They don't like educated blacks or northern "boys" because they never had the chance to be educated, although their intuitive intelligence is likely no less. They find reasons to explain why they are always being "screwed" by the system, the government, the boss, the DMV, and a host of others real and imagined.

If these sound like the same sort of problems found in South Central Los Angeles or Southeast Washington, D.C., they are. The ethnicity is different and the people they blame, but the anger and inadequacies are the same. Buddy spends time with the boy, trying to get him to make the leap it will take to get him out of this circle of anger and poverty and hate. It won't be easy to convince him, but it wasn't easy to convince Buddy many years ago. I am sure as long as Buddy and Boots stay here, he won't stop trying.

He says these are the things he thinks about these days in his chair outside the door of his Motor Coach while he watches Boots chase a ball or chew a bone. He does not believe that what he has done proves anything. Yet, the man I talked to was a man who improves the world because he worked hard and still likes and cares about the people he meets, and a sick little dog he didn't have to care about at all. Buddy believes that if you remain inquisitive about what make things work you remain intellectually stimulated. He feels if he does a good deed for someone, they might do one for someone else later on. All he asks in return for his many kindnesses is that you remember that.

If I meet just a few more people like Buddy, I will have had a fruitful journey.

SEVEN

PENSACOLA, FLORIDA

There is nice weather here. They need rain badly and have had very little. No air-conditioning is needed even this far south. There is a pleasant breeze and low humidity. It is about 87 degrees in the daytime and we had a low of 57 the night I got in. A pleasant campsite on a "lake" with all manner of ducks and geese and a kindly owner hosted me during this stay. He races a pair of geese in his golf cart every morning. When he appears to be winning the geese cheat by flying. It is pretty funny to watch. He thinks it great sport and looks forward to it everyday.

I hope I caught everyone's e-mails. My host gracefully provided my electronic access by running an extension cord and a 30-foot phone wire to the storage shed when he realized the office had steps.

This is a stop that will be quite personal. The things I see will stir many memories. Some of these stories have been told before and some have not. Those who know these stories are old and, sadly, some who knew them best are dead. They were special people in my life and played a huge part in my growing up. Maturity came to me eventually, as it does to most of us if we live long enough. To the extent that it came any quicker to me than it would have naturally, it was because of the time I spent in this southern Navy town where they first disabused me of my individuality, then taught me about trusting others, and finally taught me how to fly. I had come now to see places and remember deeds during my short and vainglorious Navy career. The people and places I saw here were involved in some of it. Two of the "survivors" helped me bring it into focus. If I digress from this place then, it is only in memory of the times we shared elsewhere and were made more vivid for having seen these places and people again.

I traveled to the main base of the Naval Air Station Pensacola very early the first morning. The Marines at the gate are still as ramrod straight and as polite as there always were. Perhaps they were more polite today at 5 AM to a man in a van waving a retired military ID card. They are children, of course. They were not even born when I was here as an Aviation Officer Candidate. Perhaps their fathers stood where they do now and saluted the blue decal on the front bumper of our flashy cars as we, of perhaps the same or lesser age, nodded sagely and went through the gate at the signal to do so. Today there are questions about where I am going and a day pass issued to permit me to have my vehicle on the base. But in the end, there is still the quiet "yes sir" from a Lance Corporal, and the privilege of a salute. Oddly, I never found saluting those of lesser rank, or being saluted by them while walking around very important. I thought it a bit silly and pompous in some ways. But when a gate guard saluted me in my car or a plane captain saluted me as we taxied from the flight line or down the carrier deck, it was a rush. I get the same rush as my vehicle passes now. The Navy tradition does not permit a return salute while in a vehicle. So when these Marines snap smartly to attention and salute, a wave of the hand or an attempt to look sage while giving a small nod of the head is what one does. Perhaps this lack of a need to respond and yet in a way let them know that you acknowledge it is what makes it special. Perhaps it is because they were doing it because they could tell by the flashy car that you might be one of those with the "Right Stuff." This is and was then the "Cradle of Naval Aviation." These ceremonials are perhaps silly, but they have been done this way for more time than I have been on this earth and tradition will not permit me any other response.

I make my way to the area of the base were the boot camp barracks are. They are in the same place as those that I used 34 years ago and the morning formation and inspection was forming in the street in front of the three Georgian style brick structures that housed the company of cadets.

They are in the uniform appropriate for the weather of the day; tropical tans and low-quarter blacks. In English, it means they are wearing khaki trousers and short-sleeved shirts open at the neck and highly polished black shoes of ankle height. They all knew this was the uniform, that the above ankle "boondockers" were not to be worn, and no raincoats were to be worn or carried because it had been posted on the bulletin board last night and the Battalion Cadet Officer of the Day (BCOD) had confirmed it on the loudspeaker when Reveille was sounded at 0430. That is the last chance to give information that might have changed from the night before. One learns to wake quickly to hear such things, since, had rain come during the night, as it will in this Gulf Coast town, the Plan of the Day (a.k.a. the POD) posted the night before would have made the information on it about a uniform or place of the inspection obsolete. With only five minutes to dress and ready oneself for inspection, time is not wasted. The BCOD was a cadet from a class somewhere midway through the sixteen-week ordeal known as Boot Camp. It was his responsibility to pass on new information at this, the earliest opportunity.

On one occasion during my time here, reveille sounded during a rain. The unfortunate fellow on duty forgot to include a few essential facts in his announcement of reveille, which, to even a second week recruit, was obvious, but since not changed, remained the POD. He did not tell us that the inspection was to be held indoors at our cubicles rather than in a very wet street. He also failed to tell us that the shoes to be worn had been changed and raincoats were to be carried or worn if required.

Since there are three buildings, there are three BCODs; we lesser beings presumed that the others had made a change. Loud protests began being hooted up and down the passageways and ladder wells toward the poor young man. Embarrassed and choking on his voice since he was never sure the Battalion Drill Instructor was not just down the hall at this early hour, ready to correct him in his unique way. He finally handed the microphone to an assistant, an even more junior cadet that had nursed the Battalion through this very short night, who announced the change. It would be nice to report that this was a character building experience for this young, soon to be commissioned fellow, but alas, it was not. Since not in my "week", thus not my Boot Camp class, I did not know him well, but I did know him to be a pretty good cadet. After he had been verbally "ripped" by Cadet Officer's and the Sergeant, he was put on report and assigned tours to march on Saturday morning for the age-old Navy crime known simply as "Screwing up." He dropped out about two weeks later and went to the fleet as a "Dixie Cup." This was our not so flattering term for those who did not complete either Boot Camp or Basic Flight Training and served the rest of their tour as enlisted men wearing the traditional Navy white hat which, when viewed from a certain angle, looks exactly like the container of that name. Busy as we all were, we shrugged and decided that he really did not want to fly all that bad after all or he just didn't have it. In retrospect, I am sure it was a crushing blow to a young man who may have dreamt of flying all his life. At the time, we were too busy to be so gentle or introspective in our judgment. If someone dropped out while we endured this frenzied pace, they were simply forgotten. They were no longer a part of the everyday life full of tension and pressure, so they were irrelevant. And, although we might see them around the base for a week or two while they awaited orders, they ceased to exist.

On this beautiful spring morning in a new century the formation looked as neat and rigid as I recalled it. There was a singular and startling difference. Nearly a third of those now standing at rigid attention in the street awaiting inspection, questions, and minor verbal abuse from this week's Cadet Officer's, were women. How odd. I had forgotten. I expected, I suppose, to hold up a mirror and see a reflection of 34 years ago. Instead, I saw today's Navy, where Aviation Officer Candidates come, not only in most sizes and shapes, but now of both sexes as well. A few moments later, a Cadet Officer approached and asked if there was something that I needed. When I turned, I saw the sharp creased khakis and the three bar emblem of a Cadet Battalion Commander. She seemed quite pleasant, but had that clear, firm sound of command in her voice. I said no. I told her I was only here to try to remember what it was like to be that young, believe I was that smart, and have that much energy so early in the morning. She looked at me, smiled a smile that made my day and decided, I suppose, to accept that I was not a danger to her or others, and after a moment of small talk about what plane one flew and war one might have been in, which had a lot of "sirs" spread through it, she moved on with a military bearing many of my colleagues would have envied.

When the inspection ended, the ranks marched off in the general direction of the Mess Hall or elsewhere to begin the long, sometimes cruel day that would end at 10 PM that night with "Taps."

Each class, from week two through fourteen is on different schedules. In week fifteen, the week before your last, you are out in the Florida swamp learning the rudimentary techniques of escape and evasion and how to cook tea from Palmetto leaves. Such skills would be refined with far more horrid experiences, should you "reach the fleet", that is, graduate and complete flight training.

In your last week, you are in "charge" as a "Cadet Officer." The rank you have determines your duties, but even more importantly, the rank you have is determined by the ranking of your peers as well as your academic and physical training marks. Each week, we graded the three highest cadets in our class. A large part of it is for selflessness and teamwork. It is a good system. Oh, I am sure there are those who picked someone because they were friends, but in my time, it was usually the guys that came in from liberty and waxed the floors in the common areas on a Sunday night instead of catching a nap. At least that is how I rated them. It was one of the reasons why I had been impressed by the lady I had just met. She held the second highest rank a Cadet Officer could hold. There were only three Battalion Commanders. Her athleticism and academics had to be good enough, but more importantly, her peers had to think her good enough to rank her that high. This both surprised me and is testament perhaps that the Navy ethos was truly changing.

When the morning formations had dispersed, I drove to the most impressive Naval Aviation Museum. As a sign of my age, perhaps, it contained every plane I had ever flown and some pictures and exhibits of familiar scenes and faces. It is a most impressive place. It is a reminder of how proud Naval Aviation is of its' history and its' many extraordinary heroes.

I left the base after lunch and handed my pass to the guard. He took it, and in a gesture of kindness, stiffened and snapped off one more perfect salute, which gave a gray haired man driving a van with handicapped plates, one last thrill. I nodded sagely and went on.

-2-

I had come also to see some of my former aviator colleagues who have retired here. Many come back here who have made the Navy a career. I went through part of advanced flight training with one of them and through a war with the other. The first graduated the Naval Academy. He is a funny man originally from the West Coast with whom a few fellow bachelor officers and I shared a house during advanced training in Key West, Florida. He introduced me to the ugly but delicious avocado, and the strange looking vegetable that one peeled the leaves from and dropped in butter and then sort of ripped through your teeth. I still find the artichoke a little too strange. He also showed me how to make frozen daiquiris in mason jars.

Together one hot Saturday morning we assembled a scooter in the front yard of the rented house. The scooter had come from his family when he sent a letter telling them how incredibly boring a place Key West could be in the summer. It arrived in a box and about twenty paper bags and had about a one horsepower engine. It was not a registered vehicle in the state of Florida or anywhere else. Undaunted by such legalities, we planned a household competition to see who could ride it the farthest without getting stopped by the police. It stood about three feet off the ground so it takes little imagination to picture a grown man (physically grown, that is), in a bathing suit and flip flops, knees out to the side and arms akimbo roaring down the sidewalk or street on this contraption. It had neither a muffler to quiet the ear splitting din nor anything to dampen the blue smoke from its' two-stroke lawn-mower engine that mixed the oil and gasoline together. We found that night was best for "test" rides. The lack of a light on the "vehicle" and our 20/20 or better vision and guile made us, we were sure, unstoppable. The scooter was nicknamed "Mach." Our trips on it were usually three blocks to the beach and back in the early evening when no one much cared about it. The redoubtable owner used to don fins and a snorkel mask for the trip, which made it a funny enough sight to even the most callous neighbor so he was left pretty much alone.

There were a group of Peace Corps volunteers training at an elementary school nearby for assignment in Micronesia. Obviously, the Florida Keys was a good venue to approximate the eventual destination. The climate was right and there were Keys that had access only by water. Unfortunately, Micronesian volunteers were sort of hybrid since they were actually going to an American possession and, in one of its' few lapses in good judgment, the Peace Corps took about anyone who volunteered without much screening. Or at least that is how the Navy folks had heard it. So here on this very hot, small island paradise we had steely-eyed fighter pilots and weapons officers, and a group of unscreened young folks who did not think much of warriors. A textbook definition of the reaction of oil and water could not have been better written.

Since they were involved in group activities most of the time, and we were now in our primary aircraft in what was known as the Replacement Air Group learning the plane and refining our skills, our opportunities to terrorize them were abundant. "Mach" and its' owner used to make regular evening "low passes" through the schoolyard where classes were in session on his way to the beach. They were not amused and by association considered the rest of us who lived in the house psychopathic and worse. Socialization was, therefore, out of the question. Attempts to even say hello were often rebuffed. That was too bad. The single men outnumbered women (if military dependents were not counted) by a factor of three during the months when we were there since the contract schoolteachers were not on the island. There were some women in the group I would not have minded meeting. Harassing volunteers was also not something I generally considered a sport, since I had dated one in college who would later spend two years in the Philippines. This group was strange enough, however, and we were close enough to going to see real bullets and missiles that we reacted to each other in the worst possible way. A peace sign on a forehead and shoulder length hair were still unusual to those of us that led a sheltered military life in 1965. Nothing serious ever happened aside from a great deal of yelling when we drove by, or the occasional stream of epithet coming from the classrooms when a "low pass" was performed. It all seems quite tame now, but my roommate had started it so we all felt compelled to defend the honor of the Navy and the right to ride an unregistered, un-muffled midget scooter anywhere we pleased. So on the evenings he was flying, one of us would make the trip.

One evening, in a haze of frozen margaritas, the five of us determined that anyone who managed to drive the scooter to the bar in town we usually hung out in and back to the house—which was about the limit of the fuel for "Mach"—would be awarded "The Order Of The Scooter, with Combat Cluster." If you have ever participated in decision making in that state, you know how absolutely right and just it seems at the time.

I came home late from a cross-country flight one Friday evening pretty annoyed that the plane had broken and we had to land in northern Florida to get it fixed. I was hungry. I was very thirsty. The margaritas were already gone as were my roommates. I had been scheduled to go to Miami that afternoon to spend the weekend in the company of members of the opposite sex. I had missed the trip. When I found "Mach" propped up against the steps of the house, I decided to go to the aforementioned bar where I assumed some of my roommates could be found, holding court for the few local "dollies" (They were actually called that in those much less politically correct times). Even in light of my sobriety, but likely because of my utter disgust with being stuck one more warm and humid night on the island at the bottom of the United States, I decided to take the honors offered me by our noble scooter.

So, over sidewalks, through shrubbery and backyards as well as a substantial part of the main street I went, sounding like a broken lawnmower and looking a bit like a turtle. I had planned a route earlier in an idle moment and it worked. I achieved the grounds of the bar and, as luck would further have it, someone opened the door just as I came in the parking lot. Without further thought and to get a "confirmed sighting" to assure my status as the Scooter Ace, I went through the door spewing blue smoke and horrific noise. I made a circuit of the dance floor, to a standing ovation, and headed home on a different street. I was able to drop the scooter, nearly dry of fuel now, in the back yard of our nearest neighbor before sprinting to the beach in the late evening just to be elsewhere when the Key West police inevitably showed up.

They did, but no one was home and the scooter was not near the house so, remarkably, they left. "Mach" remained with us for the rest of our time there.

Sometime later, in a much less sober state, I was awarded the Order of the Scooter. It may have been the stupidest trick, and the proudest moment in my career up to that time. I became a folk hero for a week or so in the squadron, and, even excused from Margarita-making duty by the senior officers of the house for a time. There was some resentment that I had done the deed while sober, but with the whimsy and the testosterone driven spirit we all possessed at the time, I dismissed such criticism, and to anyone in earshot, proclaimed that I was now not only The Greatest Naval Aviator Who Ever Lived, but also The Best Scooter Driver in The Free World. Humility, or lack of hyperbole, does not flourish in the mind of a fighter jockey.

Most of us from that house were scheduled to go to the same squadron on the East Coast. The vagaries of the Bureau of Naval Personnel, however, sent some one way and some the other. I got orders West and my scooter building friend stayed in the East. He retired as a Captain (full Colonel for you who do not translate ranks from the arcane Navy to the "uniform services") after a distinguished career.

The other "inmate" I saw from the asylum is a retired Admiral who grew up in the Bronx and was the Commander of an aircraft carrier. He also commanded other things before going to do Pentagon things. He is still a New Yorker in manner, speech, and humor. He was a bit less crazy than the rest of us, which is why I believe he made Admiral. There are stories about him, but none so whimsical since we did not meet until we had gone to war

He had tortured me with two-hour "ready deck" watches in the middle of the night. It was his job in the squadron to make out the watch and flight schedules. He did it well and he was fair. Unfortunately, the rules, quite unspoken, required him to give the "graveyard" side of the two hour times we would sit in the plane waiting to be launched in case the carrier was attacked to the most junior officers. I was certainly the most junior of those so I logged a lot of seat time in the middle of the night. He did it all with as much fairness as the unwritten rules allowed. He also did everything with a wit that defied our circumstance.

When I was first injured, he was the one who took care of my Mother. He met her plane and drove her where she needed to go and made sure she had what she needed. He made the words about the Navy being a big family real. He is a Prince and had been one of the few non-Academy graduate Aviators I knew who went out of his way to get extra training when we were aboard the ship. He wanted to know how it worked, because he knew he was going to make it his career, even if he never bothered to mention it to us. When the squadron returned from its' next sea duty long after I had left town, he made sure I made it to the party by nearly kidnapping me. There may have been a kinder soul, but I did not know one at the time.

One still flies and as it turns out, experiments with gliders of all things. It is a long way from Mach 2. I had been in a glider once in California and found it like sailing, a silent and interesting experience. In that case we had been launched from the Torrey Pines Glider Port, or such as it was at the time, so no tow was required. On this Saturday, I was unceremoniously dumped in the cockpit of a two-seat glider. You get to ride in front as the passenger for reasons that have to do with the center of gravity and not worth explanation. I mention it here only to let you visualize being towed heavenward at the end of a rope, with no control over anything. You go high enough to catch a thermal updraft and the powered craft releases the tow to let you wander around on the wind, hopefully up, until you run out of time or "good air." It is a lovely way to see the landscape and much more controlled and safer than it sounds. The landing was better than I remember, when "arriving" on the aircraft carrier in a Phantom. We laughed a lot more on the way in, too.

In this very short visit, I ate a lot of good seafood, enjoyed some memories good and bad, much laughter, a few tears, and recalled many good times with people from another life. It was good to see at least two of them. They were characters in what seemed like a play for me since my career was so short. They were merely two of some of the more interesting people I met during a time of my life when I finally began to understand the difference between existence and taking responsibility and learning how to lead others. These two had helped me learn it. For that I am forever grateful.

EIGHT

GADSDEN, ALABAMA

I drove 325 miles today and did most of it early since there were some side trips. It is a cool and overcast day. I may finally be catching up with some of the rain that I have missed thus far.

This is a pleasant town. To get here from Pensacola, you drive the first 80 miles on U.S. 29, which for a short stretch in Alabama, is known as the "Don Sutton Highway." Yes, baseball fans, Don Sutton the Dodger pitching great who was the other part of the Koufax, Drysdale combination in the early years in Los Angeles, and now the announcer for the Atlanta Braves, was born in the Alabama town of Clio and has that section of U.S. 79 named after him. I am not sure it is a great honor, but until he was inducted into the National Baseball Hall of Fame in 2000, it may have been one of the few he had.

Historians cannot agree on how Alabama came to be named. There was a theory, now largely disproved, that it meant " Here We Rest". This is the responsibility of one Alexander Beauford Meek who wrote prodigiously in the 1850s. It is also claimed to have been a word from the Muskogee Indians. No one has been able to locate the word derivation however, so it is now pretty much accepted that it is one of many spellings of an Indian word used by early English, French, and Spanish chroniclers. One of the major waterways in the state derived its name from the group as well. There is a very convoluted explanation of all this in the local visitor handouts which includes the penchant for the early Indian languages for commonly substituting *m* for *b*. There is even a later version from the Choctaw language which sort of suggests that the word was once two and meant, when taken together "thicket clearers". Whatever the case, there it is. The territory, now the two states of Alabama and Mississippi, was then one and the border between the two was a surveyed line done at the behest of the state legislature.

The War Between the States colors much of the early history here, since after the war or during it, a number of places changed names, often on the same day. This was the Capital of the Confederacy where Jefferson Davis attempted to run a badly organized country that believed in States Rights and the War at the same time. County Government also was the most important unit for many years and the locals still talk in those terms. Thus, when one tries to learn about Gadsden as a City, it is sometimes referred to as the "seat of Etowah County", and not as an entity itself. That county, by the way, was created in 1866 and originally known as Blaine, named after a Confederate General. The State Constitutional Convention in 1868 abolished it on December 1st and created Etowah later the same day and Gadsden was made the county seat of government. It is a bit like following Alice through the Looking Glass just to find out where it all started.

After an all too brief hiatus on Sutton Highway and some other secondary roads, the trip required the use of I-65 and then north on I-59. These "I" roads are also all named for someone or some group. They are "memorial" highways in most cases. Sutton seems to be one of the few who have achieved the honor while alive. Alabama seems to have a great number of these, although many of the states no do it as a visible way to honor veterans groups, war memorials and people of some stature born within their borders.

One of the things that strikes you when looking through the information that the visitor centers give out and at a website for the state, is the number of famous people born here. Sutton may be one of the least well known. Henry Aaron, also a pretty fair baseball player, was born here. Tallulah Bankhead, an actress and later a Hollywood columnist of great renown in the last century, Kate Jackson and Jim Nabors, Zelda Fitzgerald and Truman Capote, Fanny Flagg and Helen Keller, Nat "King" Cole and Jimmy Buffett, W.C. Handy and Lionel Ritchie, Willie Mays and Mel Allen, Hank Williams and Tammy Wynette, Bo Jackson and Joe Louis. It seems like a lot of disparate and truly great talent to have come from such a sparsely populated place.

There are more and the State has various "Hall Of Fame" designations for the categories they represent. There is also a state "Hall of Fame" which is the big time. Oddly, Booker T. Washington is the only African American in that group and it appears they stopped electing people to the overall Hall in the 1950's. There is no explanation of why. Perhaps those who decide such things have found no others they deem worthy of the honor.

I stopped briefly in Selma where I worked at a hospital for a weekend during the troubles at the Edmund Pettis Bridge many years ago. The Order of Priests who ran my college in Vermont run a hospital there, as well as other missions in this part of the south. The hospital took in the people injured when the Sheriff of Selma at the time, one "Bull" Connor, decided he didn't want Martin Luther and his friends to walk across "his" bridge on the way to Montgomery during a very large protest. I was in the Navy nearby and came by to help out. I didn't tell the Navy about it at the time. I figured it was better not to get them upset about the fact that one of their expensive Aviation trainees was taking a little leave to help bandage heads made bloody by the Selma Police. I thought they had more important things to worry about.

Birmingham brought me to "Liberty Park" both for lunch and to see the replica of the Statue of Liberty that is there. It is the real Lady and an imposing site. The park is a beautiful place to be on a cool day in May. It may seem an odd place for such a monument to some, but they are very proud of her here and her idyllic setting. I had a picnic lunch on the grounds and watched people stroll the vast lawn and eat under the sprawling trees. This is a time of the year and a venue that makes the south seem a wonderful place.

Gadsden is one of those southern cities that people pass through and don't realize how much history is attached. It is the seat of the county government and at the base of the Appalachians. My campsite tonight is on a river that feeds Weiss Lake. Many of the campgrounds are on rivers or streams. I suspect there are dozens just in this area that have the word river in their name, but few are this pretty or as real. Many are also close enough to the railroad tracks here in the south to hear the wail of the whistle at night. One doesn't have to wonder why so many country songs have wailing train whistles somewhere in the lyrics if you have gone camping in the south.

Ducks and geese are flourishing and families of various ages are marching about the bank with Mom and Dad. None fly yet, so the elders keep a close eye on them, and a not too darn friendly eye either if you are trying to get close enough to take a picture. Some of these little guys (okay, goslings) could not have been more than a week or two old.

Bass is the catch of the day. Lots of people are fishing and some are actually catching. This river has speedboats, which disturbs the whole thing now and again. The place also is the first campground to have a chapel on site. It is about as big as my van and is named "Ruth's Chapel". It was built in memory of the original owner. The current owners will tell you about it and her for a good while if you happen to ask. Apparently she was the wife of the original owner and quite religious. She also thought that it would be nice to have a place for people to contemplate if they wanted to. Now the group there the night I stayed didn't look all that contemplative and I didn't see anyone actually go in it but me, but who knows? It may not be a bad idea at all.

It seemed that the fishing and the boating opportunities attracted a few seasonal renters who had already moved in. Some folks looked like they had been here awhile and had boats and all terrain vehicles and all manner of "toys" about their campsite. There was a large Latino family down the way that had a great time fishing most of the afternoon, actually catching a few fish and having a noisy dinner outside under the threatening skies that night. It smelled very good and they sounded like they had fun.

Tomorrow I will spend two days at the foot of the Great Smoky Mountains. It was cool up there, 65-70, when I spoke to a campground owner yesterday. I am still very much looking forward to this part of the trip since I get to go wherever I want, and camp almost anywhere in the park and along the Blue Ridge Parkway. I will return to civilization in a place called Front Royal Virginia, well north of Roanoke and south of Gettysburg.

As sleep comes, so do dark clouds and the first real threat of rain.

NINE

PIGEON FORGE AT KNOXVILLE, TENNESSEE

The trip here from Gadsden started ugly and stayed that way. I thought it would rain, so I was up early to clear the outside connections before it did so I wouldn't have to slosh around in the mud. That probably had me moving faster and thinking less clearly. I have not yet learned that it does not matter if it rains. It does not matter if I leave later than a time I have decided is a "good" time. It is all very simple. You put on the rain gear, do what you have to do and decide whether you want to drive now or later. Having rainwater on your hat is not like a jail sentence or anything. It just happens, then it dries and it is all over. One day I may understand these things better. Mud is not fun, but it wasn't a muddy site that I was parked in, so I would have had to work to get muddy.

There was the matter of unhooking the water. I managed to release the quick release on the van without first turning off the water or loosening the connection at the pipe. This is not a hard thing to remember and releasing this way is not that easy, although I will not do it again just to prove that theory. Who knows what I was thinking about? The hose took off like a snake being charmed by music. It even managed to turn on me. Rain began as I suspected it would. I dried off and managed to get on the road without further incident, humbled once again by a simple mechanical device.

As I moved northeast, a merciless downpour began that lashed the van all day until I reached the turnoff for the next place to stay. It broke into showers there long enough for me to get hooked up at a campsite along the Little Pigeon River here in Pigeon Forge, Tennessee. This is a huge campground and is really the last town of any size before you head uphill into The Smoky Mountain National Park. The minor league ballpark of the Knoxville Smokies is right down the road. It appears new. They are on a road trip so I missed them. They are a Class AA franchise, of the Toronto Blue Jays so I doubt I would have recognized many names. But it would have been a ballgame, nonetheless. I am taking an extra day to remember that I am now in the Eastern Time Zone and do some of the chores of life—haircut, laundry, and groceries, sorting out some questionable contents in the refrigerator and organizing laundry. I was unloading e-mail and picking up messages at the office when I asked about a supermarket. One of the owners told me of a shopping center and said if I went there I could go to the bank, have someone do my laundry for me, shop and get my hair cut. There were even two restaurants so I could eat dinner on the way out. It was in fact a full service shopping mall and I was delighted since I only had to park the van once.

I have been reading some of the literature the campsite hands out about the attractions in the area. I must say surprise does not begin to cover it. The area here just outside the park is an odd mix of cultures. There are a few areas that are housing developments and may be suburbs of Knoxville, but more obvious is the vacation atmosphere because it is near the Park. There are campgrounds and motels of all types and prices, flea markets, all year round Christmas ornament and decoration shops, lots of "antique" shops, fast food of every kind. This all huddles at the base of the mountain outside the Park, as if it is time to get the last tourist bucks before they go in and be sure they are here at night when they come out. The most surprising, to my innocent mind, is a cottage industry in "theaters" that include one for a Mandrell sister I have never heard of and Lee Greenwood among others. Dolly Parton is clearly the big draw. If you are a Dolly Parton fan, I am sorry, but I found none of what I saw of any social redeeming value or tasteful either on her part or those that sell the trinkets and photos of the blond lady who, by now, is old enough to know better.

There is a place called Dollywood. It is loosely defined as a park along the lines of Six Flags. It has more, than that, or less, depending on how you view things. There is bus and trolley service to this monument to bad taste from nearly all the motels. Everyone who comes here goes there. They treat it like Graceland. The difference is Dolly and her business enterprise profit from everything in this little spot of "heaven" whereas in Memphis, Graceland is but a building surrounded by many tacky shops not directly associated with Presley Enterprises. I have not seen such a collection of strange things, people and outfits since I went to Graceland. There are videos of Dolly, there are shows "produced" by Dolly, there are dinner shows one can attend while a 32 horse performance occurs right before your very eyes, and your table, if you are lucky enough to be up close. There is a lot more; water rides of every description, crafts that allege to keep the "old" ways of doing things alive, like knife making, woodcarving, and sand casting. It is advertised that one can actually go there and build a Dulcimer, which is a miniature piano by any other name. Now, how many times would you have to go there to do that? You can stick your head through a cardboard cutout and have your picture taken and look just like Dolly with a guitar and boots and a tastefully fringed western outfit. There are an awful lot of people who look like Dolly there already. But, alas, there is no Dolly. She apparently shows up once or twice a year (boy, wouldn't it be special to be here for that?) to legitimize the whole operation and justify the Foundation status. This pleases her legion of fans so much that there is apparently no room at any Inn or campsite for many miles around.

I guess I understand the need to idolize someone. I am unclear on why each of us chooses those that we make larger than life. I must admit that Dolly never entered my mind as someone to put in my personal pantheon. Others obviously have and embraced her. There are some men, but mostly women, mostly middle aged and older, most overweight and with some version of a Dolly hairstyle and enough makeup on their face to make you sure a strong breeze might knock them over if the didn't have such weight in steerage. I wonder if I would find the same idolatry and trinket shops should I pass through Independence, Missouri near the Truman Library? Of course not, and that is what troubles me about idols of choice. People like Truman, or the early suffragettes like Elizabeth Cady Stanton, and FDR and a host of others do not draw these sweaty palmed matrons ready to plunk down twenty bucks for a CD the alleges to have a song "never before released" on it. It makes me wonder about priorities, society, and in general, what people truly admire.

To be fair to Dolly Parton, this is run for the benefit of a charity (although the overhead to actual benefit figures are not easily found) which "develops and administers" educational programs for the children of Sevier County where it is located and where Dolly was born. But fair or not it is hyperbole I think to characterize it as "the playground of the south."

Well, toys for the idle mind to ponder. Dollywood will be left behind tomorrow. Soon enough, I will find some other offense to my sense of good taste. Or, with luck, I will be able to offer more positive social commentary.

I have treated this stop since the beginning of the trip as the beginning of the real camping. It is as if I have reached base camp at Mount Everest and will provision myself for the trip up the great slope and employ my Sherpa guides in the way of Edmund Hilary. It is as if there is a break in the pace of the trip that comes here, that all before has been knocking about in small towns of interest but that this is the real reason I drove this far. It is not true. I cannot explain why it seems so, or why the mantra of "just wait until I get to the Smoky's and the Blue Ridge" has been so strong. Maybe it is the rural nature of what I will see in the next week. There is no fast food so no quick answer when you get hungry except to fix yourself something to eat. There is no convenient electricity in the campsites. Maybe this is the ultimate solo part of the trip and I look forward to it for that reason. Perhaps the need to find my amusement in the people and places I see out in the woods is what make me anticipate it so much. I am not sure, but I hope I will know when I am finished.

There is much to see in the Smoky Mountain National Park. Those who have been here know it is organized in "loops", some of which can be driven and some of which are for hiking only. One will take you to the top of the second highest mountain east of the Mississippi River. Buddy told me he rode his motorcycle up through one area that will be my first to visit in the morning, Cades Cove. It is what is left of a once prosperous settlement in a valley near the top of the mountain. If Buddy recommended it, it must be good. It isn't something he was known to do, believing that we all should find our own places that seem to us like paradise.

There is a drizzle in the air tonight, but the Weather Channel seems to believe it will be a lovely morning. As the light fades, I watch the ducks on the Little Pigeon River, and a man with a beard as white and as long as St. Nicholas' plies its' waters in a canoe. It seems wildly amusing to me for some reason, particularly when I later see him talking to a camper that has one of those iron Reindeer they sell at the store up the road standing in what passes for a yard in the campground. He is obviously home for the evening. Maybe he's got elves working in there. It is peaceful as darkness falls and there is a lovely quiet punctuated by the sound of doves or owls every now and then, but a good night for sleeping with a sense of amusement, accomplishment. A new haircut, and clean clothes all part of being ready for the new day.

TEN

SMOKY MOUNTAIN NATIONAL PARK

The weather is as lovely as the park. The sign on the way in says it is a "biosphere park". I am not sure what that means exactly, the only other "biosphere" experience of my life was at what I believe has been proven a bogus experiment in Oracle, AZ where six people were living in an enormous glass structure along with all the plants and animals that they would need for some ridiculous time, perhaps two years. They were sealed in with great fanfare, with no reason, allegedly, to have contact with the outside world since the plants and animals within would provide them food and air. About a year later, word had it they were leaving at night and had "visitors" some weekends that brought junk food and perhaps other pleasures. Tourists paid money to look in the windows of this giant thing (and see precious little but plants). It seems the only science proven was that P.T. Barnum was right when he said there is a sucker born every minute.

But I digress. That is another story.

I made it to nearly every site that a vehicle can get to in the Park. There is a southern road that then heads east, around the South and then into North Carolina. I will travel that tomorrow to see a few things I noticed on the map before going north. I will follow my habit and get off the road for Friday and Saturday and start up the Blue Ridge Parkway on Sunday.

The Park is so natural and beautiful it is hard to describe. Those of you who have been lucky enough to have been here know what I mean. In the early morning, the sunlight is filtered through the canopy of leaves from the dense foliage of old virgin forest. In the lower elevations, where the water runs loud and strong over the boulders in the streams, men and women stand in their waders and floppy hats casting and casting again, trying to lay the fly perfectly on the water of the quiet pools near the bank to catch the fish they know is there. From the look on their faces, whether it is and whether they catch it, is secondary to the trying and just being in this beautiful place.

The early morning was spent climbing to Cades Cove. It is an 11-mile loop of one-way road, up from about 600 feet above sea level to 3,000 feet. While it sounds as if it is at the top of a hill, it is actually a valley at the top of the mountain. There are two-way roads that leave the main loop at right angles that will take you into the meadows and woods on the way. There are horses in the pastures, and riding trails nearby. It was one of these roads, taken on a whim, where I forded a swiftly moving stream. I was so astonished that in this day and age someone would not charge admission for this. I pulled over as much as I could and got out of the van to get a better look. I decided to take a picture from the middle of the stream so I rolled happily back down the road in the cool morning. It was only as I began to move down into the water on the pavement that I began to ask myself the critical questions: How deep is it? Will the current carry me away from the road and into the streambed? And a few others I cannot now recall. I made it to midstream, and I did not seem to be moving, so took the picture and stayed awhile to enjoy the magnificent sound of the water on the rocks and stream bottom. I saw some small fish in the clear pools and likely would have sat there much longer except another car had turned in and I needed to get in the van and retract my lift or he would not be able to pass. It was a wonderful hour spent immersed in nature. Happily I was not submerged in it. I began to think that maybe this was the big deal that I had made of all this, this ability to sit surrounded by nothing but the sights and sounds of nature. I heard no cars, saw no faces and tried to identify birds I heard and saw. Maybe this was the reason for my Mount Everest mentality.

Even at this early hour and time of year, there were numerous cars on the single lane road. The first deer seen in the meadows brought all vehicles to a stop and everyone leaping out with cameras at the ready. It was an amazing Pavlovian reflex to the sight of an animal in the wild. Here, in the meadows, the deer are not tame and remain wary of these humans swarms. Little did this hoard of people know that a little further down the road there were doe that one could almost walk up and touch. I found the skittish, wilder ones more interesting. They will appear in the road, but not stay very long. The tamer ones, those fed by the tourists, will stay in a road all day if they happen to feel like it, or just start to walk up to a window looking for a handout.

The sight of the latter ones reminded me of a roommate from college who, in order to impress the lady he had with him at the time, caught a moose in the headlights crossing a road. It froze. Undaunted; our Lothario drove his MG sports car not only up to, but under the moose. The hood was warm; the moose liked that, so he or she sat down. Only a blaring horn finally got it to move and then only after substantial damage to the car.

Some of the drivers I saw today looked capable of that. Odd, but when in a Park such as this, a Nation's Park, there are many who act as if it is an amusement attraction and not at all subject to the whims of nature and the creatures around them. Some, who would stop short for a dog on their own street at home, think the deer should just get out of the way up here. They are in a hurry, although it is hard to imagine why in such bucolic surroundings. They blow a horn or yell out the window. It seems such odd behavior. I guess it is an example of people who are impatient with anything that they do not consider worthy of watching and consider it a "good time." They are in a hurry to have a good time and this "thing" is holding them up because it is not on their agenda today.

Before 1819 this area was part of the Cherokee Nation. The cove was known by an Indian name, "Tsiyahi" which meant "'River Otter'". Otters and Black bears have been reintroduced into the park, but are not seen in these early hours nearly as often as the deer. There were elk and eastern Bison there too, once, but most had been hunted out before the whites decided to settle it. The Cherokee integrated well with the Europeans and attended schools, built log and frame houses and by 1820 had a written language. They owned slaves and plantations. In 1830, the census showed that they owned over 1,000 slaves.

Unfortunately, the white man found them a nuisance, perhaps because they were so successful. Many wanted all the Indians moved west of the Mississippi River. Once gold was discovered on Cherokee lands in Georgia, and Andrew Jackson became President, the first from "rural America", the tragic migration began. It is known as the "Trail of Tears." It was another example of how greed rules the world and the imperviousness of the whites toward the Native American. More than 14,000 Cherokees left the Appalachian lands in 1838. Less than 10,000 of them reached Oklahoma. A few were hidden in the mountains by friendly whites and in the 1870's managed to reclaim some of their land in western North Carolina.

By 1850, 685 men, women, and children lived in Cades Cove. There were five roads that led to what is now Townsend Tennessee so they were not as isolated as it appears today. Oddly, these folks largely supported the Union during the Civil War and were harassed by their neighbors who did not. When the war was over they went back to their rural lifestyle, but the American expansion westward sent some of them off in pursuit of dreams and new land, and the population never again reached the level of 1850. Many left for hourly wage jobs in the logging industry and Alcoa opened a plant down the road and many left for that. Once the Park was established the outward migration continued until they simply were not there anymore. In what is something of a tradition in this country, one man stayed. I guess to prove the point that he couldn't be pushed out. Ken Caughron, the last resident did not die until 1999. He was 89 and, it is said, tough as a nail.

I am sure there is an explanation for the use of the word Cove in the name, but I never learned it. It is named for an Indian Chief (Kade) who laid claim to part of the area. One can only imagine what a difficult place it must have been to get to, some 5,000 feet off the valley floor. Left behind are the structures in which the people lived, kept their livestock, milled their lumber, and prayed. They lived poorly and harshly, died young, and often alone in this place of quiet beauty so far away. That is the wonder of it. They lived way up here. It was not an easy commute to Townsend, despite the five roads that ran in and out. Perhaps they just wanted to get away from the people below, which is the way of the hill people hereabouts. They cleared the land, lived in log houses, built barns off the ground on stilts, to avoid the spring run off or the winter snows and to store hay under in the summer. It seems even now, so far away from everyone and everything. One can only suppose they preferred it that way. This was virgin forest and a black loam soil a true farmer would love. It was here for them to take and so they did.

One could try to describe this Park forever and never get it right. To say it is a natural wonder and beautiful seems such pitiful praise. I went to The Dome on the next loop to about 7,200, feet. It is the first, second or third highest point east of the Mississippi River depending on the source you read. It was shrouded in mist and clouds. People around me kept saying they could see a lake. I had binoculars and saw no such thing this day. I read about a woman, wife of the railroad president named Vanderbilt, who saw a lake up this way and because of the odd way the water spouted around the rocks, named it Fontana, the Italian for "fountain." But I did not see it. I will look for it on the route I have planned for tomorrow. I did see sun on hillsides below and mist-shrouded valleys. This unforgiving place is lovely and verdant this time of year. Some trees at the very top of the mountain have not yet fully leafed which makes for an odd sight. It is peaceful and a place where, on a day like today, one can almost understand why those who came upon it in the 1800's might be drawn to stay.

I can say that I was "on" the Appalachian Trail at least for about two miles as it crosses a number of the roads on its way to its terminus in Georgia. I didn't see anyone who looked like they had walked down from Maine, but it has been done many times, and no doubt someone was doing it then.

Tomorrow, perhaps I will learn more about these Chilhowee Indians who had names like Abraham. They may have intermarried with the settlers of the once thriving Cade's Cove, or been converted by missionaries common here in the 19th Century. There is not much written about them in the literature of the Park that I found at the hospitable Visitor's Center.

It is hard to leave and go back to a campsite at the end of the day. There is more to this place that I will not have time to see. The Vanderbilt House and many other attractions will be missed. There is much more here to see on foot more loops on dirt roads and paths, but the hilly terrain does not lend itself to wheelchair travel. The footpaths are impossible

It was a wonderful place to visit. I hope the other Parks are as well run and kept up as this one. Those who care for this one obviously do so as a labor of love. It has been a relaxing time discovering places where people lived at a rational pace. It was a hard life, but the beauty of where they chose to carve out that life must have made up for some of that. This early in the season, the number of vehicles in the Park is still rational, as are the visitors. I know that as summer comes that will change. At present, these are not accidental tourists; they are profession-als with some day trip people mixed in. Most generally know how to move slowly and enjoy the sight of a hawk circling, or a deer foraging. Soon many who do not know the difference will be here, so it is a good time to have come and a good time to go.

ELEVEN

LOST AND FOUND IN THE CAROLINAS

My trip here was lovely if a bit confusing. I spent most of the morning in a state of general disorientation somewhere in western South Carolina. As is often my habit, I spent the early morning hours looking for something. While I did not find all I was looking for in my tour of the outskirts of the Smoky Mountain National Park, I saw most of it. I suppose I could have hummed "Amazing Grace" the whole morning since I spent I lot of time when it appeared I was lost and then was found. At one point, as I tried to keep moving east and then north, I was passing through Marysville, South Carolina. My nephew from Denver called on the cell phone. He was on his way to work and wanted to know where I was. I told him I was in a town called Marysville. He asked where that was and I asked him if it really made any difference. He said it probably didn't. I told him I was trying to follow some bad directions and he asked if I was lost. I asked him if that would make any difference. He laughed and decided that, given the nature of my journey, it likely did not matter at all. I told him not to worry; I would figure it all out before dark. He brought me up to date on doings in Denver and with the rest of the family and then made it to the parking lot at his office and signed off. I appreciated knowing that there were those out there wondering where I was, but it occurred to me when asked that it really didn't matter. A very different view than I would have had a few months ago.

While wandering, I found not only Lake Fontana, but also a number of other lovely lakes that are result of the Tennessee Valley Authority damming in the area. I saw some hardy souls camping in the pullouts along the side of the road and a lot of vehicles parked for the day whose owners were likely the people I saw in boats drifting lazily along the various bodies of water. I saw a "fish camp" late in the day. It is not much different than a "deer camp" for those of you familiar with that peculiar tradition. In a lovely spot along a fast moving stream, were a line of very old, rusty, very immovable travel trailers, which had been added on to here and there with a lean-to or a screened porch, or storage shed in the back. These once proud road warriors, now mere rusted hulks of their former grandeur are left to sit by the stream to be used during the fishing season. This will be their last resting place. I thought of the ice fisherman up in Minnesota and northern Michigan and the deer hunters of New England. They have places like these where men come to hang out with other men, smell bad, drink too much and play cards and cuss as they can not at home. It is some male bonding thing I have never fully understood. If they caught fish fine, otherwise it was just a place to come and sit on the porch, spit, and act anything but their age.

Some men need to do this. The ice fisherman do it in their shacks on the lake all winter, the deer hunters in the fall in New England, and these guys do it in the spring. They are the same ones who will be beached in a recliner with a remote in one hand and a beer in the other watching football on fall weekend afternoons.

It was pleasant in the late afternoon when I pulled in to the colorfully named "Mama Gertie's Place." I never did find out who "Mama Gertie" was even after asking the owner on two occasions. He was a colorful enough character to make me suspect he just made it up. He wore red suspenders over a waffle weave long underwear shirt, blue jeans and boots. When he wasn't tending to the office he was riding up the side of the hill going about his various tasks on a gas powered four-wheel All Terrain Vehicle that had been modified with a mini-truck bed. His nephew had one, and the casual labor used them when they could. The office and common area was a beautiful huge log house that served as a multi-purpose area.

The nephew had many body piercing and tattoos that are interesting, but is a nice and helpful young man as well. Just one of a new generation that thinks having a stud in your tongue is nice. The place is literally built into the side of a very steep hill. The sites are carved into it. There are wonderful hand stacked rock retaining walls everywhere. I cannot, although only 50 yards away, get to the main lodge without driving there. Okay, I could get down the hill, but I couldn't get back. The people are pleasant. The place was moderately full, but since we all lived on a terraced flat spot on the side of the mountain, it was hard to tell. It is very quiet. I met one couple that lived in California for 23 years. They came over after the owner had told them I was from there. They seemed to just want to see who this maniac was. They now live in a van about the size of mine after a brief, and from the description, unpleasant, sojourn somewhere in Florida. A Labrador retriever shares the space. They sold their house this winter and now live, all three, in this small space nearly full time. I think it would drive me insane. But I think the guy would all by himself if I needed to talk to him for more than ten minutes. This trip they do have a car along. When I asked if they towed it, since I was interested in the ability to tow with a van of my size, his wife replied that no, since it was "only" 1,000 miles, she drove it. That seemed excessive, but at least it got her out of the van for the trip.

I was here mainly to avoid the weekend traffic and have one more night of full services before going onto the Blue Ridge Parkway. Cold, wind, rain greeted me the next morning on my "day off." That was fine. I am always happy when I happen to pick the rainy days to be off the road. I spent much of the time organizing the van and fixing a few things. It also gave me an excuse to read, write, and take a nap. I have learned in my readings here that for some reason I had naively assumed that the Blue Ridge Parkway was just one long Park. It isn't. It passes through a number of National Parks on its way north. I will be on it tomorrow with no planned stops. I will reappear in Virginia, where the road ends. No reservations to make until I leave the northern end and will have to depend on the weather as to the amount of time I get to enjoy what I am hoping to be a good camping. No one I have talked to that has driven or hiked along the Parkway says anything but nice things about the scenery, the camping and the pace of the trip.

I lived near Washington D.C. for many years. There were many who would go out and drive short sections of the northern end in the Shenandoah National Park to experience the fall colors. So much so that massive traffic jams were common on fall weekends. I had never done it, likely because of that and now I would have the chance to see it from beginning to end and I was excited about getting to see something that I did not assume I would have the opportunity to again. Much of this trip has been a reminder that we ought to take the time to see things now; that we may not always catch it the next time because we never can be sure there will be a next time. I have been fortunate to have many "next times" this trip. I have been to many places I always wanted to visit or see again but never did because too many other things seemed important at the time. They probably weren't, but they seemed that way.

All of the camping is in the National Park sites, so it gets more rustic from here to my next motel stop in Pennsylvania. Should see some wondrous things. There is "a world of possibilities" out there as a character in a now forgotten movie says. I hope I get to see them all.

TWELVE

THE BLUE RIDGE PARKWAY

I was out of Asheville at what seemed a polite hour on this Sunday morning and headed for the Parkway. To the extent that I had a plan, it was to get into the park and find a campsite while leisurely enjoying the scenery. As it turned out, I enjoyed a great deal of the scenery of North Carolina but east and south of the Parkway.

The same guy who lives in the same size van as I do with "the wife and the dog" gave me the directions. I should have known. It was a pleasant side trip around some lakes and through some small towns.

It was also Mother's Day. Just finding a place that one can sit and eat food before going up onto the Parkway became a challenge. Finding fuel without a wait became one as well. It seems everyone in that neighborhood took Mom to church and then went to breakfast (and needed to buy gas on the way). Even the McDonald's lot was full. I finally got fuel and fled into the park on one of the prettiest days I remember so far and made my lunch at one of the many overlooks (one of some 100,000 such things by that name I would see before I left days later). The "overlook" can mean a wide spot, or pullout next to the side of the road or a parking area with trails leading to secluded picnic tables. By the time I left the Drive, I had seen one of nearly every shape and size. I do not know that there are actually 100,000. But by the time I left the park I was convinced that there were.

State lines do not define the park. Each National Park it passes through has its' peculiarities. The rules are different for campsites and traffic but they are generally benign with the singular exception of the Shenandoah. It is the only one you pay to get into, and the camping fees are higher than all the others (although the sites are no more elaborate), and it has some odd commercial places the rest of the Parks lack.

Along the way, there are exits down to the small towns. Some are famous. Luray Caverns, for example, is on the west side in North Carolina and the Civil War sites that Stonewall Jackson made famous while he had the Union Army pretty well perplexed, chasing him up and down the Shenandoah Valley are along both sides in Virginia. There are others with attractions both interesting and bizarre. Some of the North Carolina section has some lovely, well preserved old towns. Some, like Natural Bridge, Virginia are the most crass attempts to exploit something that, in its original state, is quite beautiful. You can't see it that way anymore because you have to go through two buildings, pass a wax museum and read the ads for the "Natural Bridge Zoo" before you get to see the rows of seats where everyone is expected to wait for a Native American and a Ranger to do a duet about how it came to be a sacred place (then I presume, not now, certainly) and how the "white man developed the site" in the early part of the last century. Certainly they are masters of the understatement there. They developed it to the point where no one can actually see the bridge from the town of Natural Bridge. Or anywhere else there is pavement for that matter.

When I was very young, my father gave me a device you could view a circle of slides through. You put a wheel of pictures in it and squinted to see the pictures. One of the wheels had the "Wonders of the World" on it. One of the wonders was the Natural Bridge in Virginia. It was quite lovely and one wondered how it had come to be formed. That is how I had remembered it all these years later, and how I had hoped to see it. Obviously, I was disappointed. I refused to pay to see a "natural" bridge. That seemed a contradiction in terms. I would have had to work my way down the steep set of ramps to get anywhere near it. There were people lined up outside the building when I pulled up, because the bridge wasn't "open" yet.

Open?

It is a thing constructed by nature and to be enjoyed for as far as I know much longer than the white man and the Indians were around. How does one "open" that? So, what I know of it is from the brochures I picked up, and I remember the wheel of pictures in the viewer from 40 years ago. It will have to do, since I refuse to spend the money for a post-card of a "rendering" by some hack painter, which appeared to be my only other option.

The campsite I chose was at a place called Buchanan. It was late. After a brief chat with a wandering fellow camper I remained inside the van in the twilight. It was chilly and I was hungry. It was peaceful, too. In the fading light deer came down into the camp to see what we were doing, and watching the birds and the chipmunks made the evening pleasant. There were tenting groups in the level below me that stayed up much later than I did. One tends to go to bed earlier in these places since there is no power but what you carry and the fresh air is a wonderful sedative. There is a peace and relaxation, too, that one finds just in the experience. I may not have been the first one to nod off, but I was not far behind.

-2-

The next two days on the Parkway were lovely for the pace of travel and the absence of many other people (the Mother's Day crowd went back to work). The weather was cool but clear and the pace of 45 MPH seemed just about right. The ride is less winding here than in the Smoky's, the elevations not quite as high or the road as steep. The green is still so intense that it hurts the eyes. This is a place of the senses, particularly sight. One can't see all that you want to and keep a van on the road (thus I learned the value of the overlook). Driving the ridgeline of two different mountain ranges is as enjoyable as anything I have experienced that has a road running through it.

I made camp for the night at Lewis Mountain in the Shenandoah National Park. Usually, in these campsites, the campers in tents and those in vans or RVs are separated. There are good reasons for this, since these mini houses tend to do things the campers find distasteful, like running the generator so the coffee maker will work. Hardly the thing a purist would consider a part of the wilderness experience. The site at Lewis Mountain was a mixed one for now since one section remained closed this early in the year, As a result I got to meet some interesting people who live very differently than those of us who travel in less a rustic way than ambling through the forest with everything we may need strapped to our backs. They walk into camp from all directions since trails, not roads have meaning for them. It was fun to watch. The very good ones put a tent up and made dinner and preparations for the night, including hanging their food from a very high tree to keep the animals away, all in about an hour. A family rolled in that had varying degrees of experience. Mom and Dad tried to put their tent up on its side. But, they came in by car and from Maryland, a few hours away. They were did not appear to be seasoned hikers.

We all visited about the site, which was less than half full. Once the sun started down the true hikers disappeared. They zipped up in the tent and were gone until morning. I guess when you walk ten miles or more, and perhaps see a bear, it makes you tired. It also, to be fair was an even more chilly night than the one before. I suspect more than one of those of us in campers turned on the Propane gas heaters just in case. The ranger I saw in the morning said it was 40 degrees. It was at least that in my tin house. By the time I found the guts to get up and make coffee the campers had either struck their tents if they were going onward, or were trying to heat water over propane burners and walking in circles to stay warm before eating and then leaving for the day. By the time I got on the road it was quiet in the site. One woman sat writing in front of her trailer and a fire as the sun burned through. It was her journal, she said. She keeps track of the animals and plants she has seen. It seemed like a noble profession.

Back on the road, I stopped soon enough to try to find food and fuel. The van was due to visit the friendly "waste facility" as the sewage dumpsite is so tastefully named. After I did that, I thought a large breakfast at this late hour would be nice at one of the Park run restaurants.

However, it seems that the Shenandoah runs their gift shops and restaurants during hours when they like. So one does not get food on an impulse. One will eat lunch between 12:00 and 2:00 PM. If you arrive at 11:30, you wait for lunch. No problem. I repair to the gift shop to perchance find a souvenir. That would be nice, but there is no one that appears to work there. There is a line of people all looking for someone to just take their money. These are the stragglers who managed to make it into the place before they stopped serving breakfast. Now, all they want is someone to just take their money so they can leave. I wandered around to watch this little drama unfold but by now had decided I was likely going down the mountain to eat, or eat whatever I had in the van rather than sit and just wait for the privilege to do so here. I also saw the menu, which seemed, as all things in the Shenandoah National Park, a bit pricey. In all, it was a strange experience.

I spent the rest of the day driving the last of this leg on what is known as Skyline Drive in northern Virginia. The Shenandoah it seems, even has its own name for the road which was known as the Parkway through the last three states. It occurs that I have seen enough of the trees and the mountains and overlooks. Sensory overload has set in after so many miles. A motel seems like a great idea and a real hot shower a true delight. I would not have missed these miles for anything, since I do not know of a place of more natural beauty in the woods. Some parts of the Green Mountains in Vermont might compare, or the

White Mountains in New Hampshire. While on this section, civilization is close if you have a need for it, and yet you feel isolated from it all when you are driving the Parkway. I may see greater wonders in the Rockies, but that is a long way from here and a long time from now. I have enjoyed the present, but three days of it has been about right.

THIRTEEN

WINCHESTER, VIRGINIA; GETTYSBURG, AND A LADY NAMED DOT

I had come out of the Parks and back to civilization. A motel room seemed an antiseptic place after the woods, but the hot shower was welcome as was the chance to stretch out. This next day of travel was over a short distance in miles but was a day long in memories and new people.

I am now north of the Mason Dixon Line. It is odd, but every time I come into Pennsylvania from Maryland, I am reminded of that historic line. Those two gentlemen surveyed it to settle a land dispute all the way from Ohio to the Atlantic Ocean, which was no mean feat in the early 1800's. Surveyors were a noble breed in the early colonies and states. George Washington started as one. Mason and Dixon certainly did a lot of work, and the fellow who put Texarkana on the map worked at it pretty hard too, although it might be argued he didn't get it quite right.

This line is quite straight making no allowance for natural boundaries such as rivers. It became, during the Civil War, and since, the division between "y'all" and "hello." It still is the demarcation for "the south" even though it seems quite far from it. One tends to think of Virginia well below Washington as the south and not Maryland. Yet during the war, had Lincoln not declared Martial Law in the state,

Maryland would surely have seceded, leaving the Union in the rather untenable situation of having a Capitol surrounded by hostile states. It is not clear that the majority of people of Maryland wanted out of the Union, but those around Baltimore and on the sparsely populated Eastern Shore of the Chesapeake did. Many Marylanders joined the Confederate Army, and many joined the Union forces. It was, like some of the western "border states" torn by the War, although only a few significant battles, such as Antietam, were fought there. So, it is one of those things where the history may be correct, but the reality today seems far from it.

I had not planned to return to Gettysburg. It was an impulse to see it again. I had been there often. My Father, on one of the more interesting vacations I remember took us there. He was an amateur Civil War historian. He had read all the books written by Bruce Canton, who wrote largely from the Union point of view. He had also diaries of soldiers and knew many of the fascinating stories of this one great massive American War. I inherited them after he died and had read many of them and was nearly as fascinated by this war of neighbors as he was.

When I lived in Washington, I could pretty much narrate the whole three day battle at Gettysburg by heart starting with the Confederate soldiers who came to town (the wrong one it turned out) looking for shoes up to and including the long and painful withdrawal of Lee and the Army of Northern Virginia and the carnage in between. Gettysburg is interesting. There are houses and working farms in the middle of the battlefield where General Pickett made his charge. The battle was never, except for some minor skirmishes on the first day, fought in the actual town. The battlefield has changed very little from what I remember. The outskirts of the town have changed a great deal. Like all interesting places there is a desire to become all things to all people. There are outlet stores, The Eisenhower Convention Center, and lots of resort hotels. When we came, the battlefield was the reason and enough. A chance to buy shoes and shirts at a discount was for another day.

The "personal tour guides" of my youth survive. They are interesting fellows who will ride along with you in your car and tell you the whole story of the battle and stop at the more important places. They know many things such as the gauge and range of the different artillery pieces and which side had how many of each. They knew many of the stories so strange to this battle and to that war, where families and friends believed so passionately about States Rights and slavery that it tore the families and the friendships apart. Here at Gettysburg, for example, the only civilian killed was the fiancée of a soldier whose company fired the shot. There was a farmer, loyal to the Union who lived here. His son was in the Confederate Army. They saw each other here for the first time in years and spent two hours in the root cellar of his house before the shelling started and the boy went back to the battle. They both survived. The house did not.

Major Abner Doubleday was here, as he had been at Ft. Sumter the day the war began and he was only a Lieutenant. He had already likely invented his form of baseball and would later build the San Francisco cable car system. There are many, many more. It is part of what haunts you about the place. It is what haunts us about that War. It was very personal to all that fought in it since it was a massive fight among people who had differences of opinion, but not of dreams, and who had common roots. Almost 55,000 men died here in three days, nearly as many as in the entire Vietnam War. This was not even the bloodiest of the battles. It is estimated that more than that died at Antietam, Maryland.

I stood again at the place where General Pickett and his 12,000 men left to cross 1,000 yards of open field under withering fire to try to breach the Union lines on the high ground. The line stretched for more than a mile. By the time they reached the Emmitsburg Road, the line was so devastated it was but one half mile long. Only 200 men actually made it to the Union line and were quickly captured or fell back. General Pickett was not one of them. The charge cost General Lee the cream of the Army. All 15 Regimental Commanders, two Brigadier Generals and six Colonels were killed.

Like many, Pickett had been to West Point and had friends in both armies. Under flags of "truce" some of his friends in the Union Army even came to visit him the night before he moved out and tried to make him understand that he could not succeed. He seemed to acknowledge that he would not when he spoke in a melancholy way about the human cost. Yet he had a duty to perform for General Lee and the Confederate States and so he led the right flank and center of the awful charge.

A battle with losses as enormous as this should have been decisive, yet, when it was over, when the southern troops had no more to give, their energy spent, the Union forces under General Meade (who had been in command of the Army less than a week), fearing a counter attack near dark and its cost, let General Lee take what he had left of his Army of Northern Virginia and re-cross the Potomac and leave, to the great agitation of President Lincoln. Meade did not press the battle, he did not try to pursue that army and kill it as he so easily could have. A seventeen-mile long wagon train left to regroup and fight again for another two years, at great cost to both sides. General Grant finally laid siege to Richmond while General Sherman burned the South and it was over. So much carnage and hate could have been avoided had Meade fought differently and decisively. So many men might have been saved. It is sad to stand there and look across the wheat fields and realize all of this. It is hallowed ground that haunts me still. After awhile I left, still sobered by the thoughts of the horror of those three days in July. The battlefield still has that effect, despite the outlet stores and the resort hotels.

-2-

I took a route out of town I was not familiar with since it headed west and I usually went east when I visited. I was wandering a two-lane road through small towns. I wanted to be sure I was headed back in the general direction of where I was spending the night. I reached a town that had one of those small beauty salons. They are always in a very small building standing alone by the side of the road. What attracted me to it was the parking area. I needed to get far enough off the road to check the map and it was long enough to get the whole van in it. A lady named Dot ran this one, and Dot decided to come out and see if I was all right, "being from California and all" as she put it. She set me straight on the route back to the main highway, and asked if I would like some ice tea. That seemed like a good idea and the town seemed interesting and there was plenty of time left in the day. I had just passed the Possum Hollow Inn, a strange and foreboding looking place not open at this time of day, and that led to some questions even if nothing else was remarkable about the place. Dot was proud to point out that her place had a ramp (it is unusual for these places), but later described several handicapped customers so her interest in access was not without pecuniary intent.

Dot was looking forward to a very quiet afternoon, "unless someone drops in on the way home from the packing plant," she said, so talking to me while smoking a pack of cigarettes seemed something to do for her at least. She even silenced the television set that had been blaring when we came in.

The town was near Mount Holly Springs where Sid Bream, a first baseman who played much of his career with the Pittsburgh Pirates came from. It said so right on the sign. He is famous for a play at the plate in the National League Play-offs with the Atlanta Braves. It was a remarkable, exciting and heartbreaking moment. Sid was on a World Series winner once. A very good ballplayer who shattered his knees early but still could hit even after all the surgery. Dot knew all about him. After all, a major league ballplayer didn't grow up around here everyday.

This place is not as large or nearly as well developed downtown as the previously described Oklahoma town; it is a suburb of nothing and supports itself with the packing plant, and a farm implement repair business. Yet the highway strip malls are where the heavy shopping gets done and the State Route I was on was the main street. Dot is the only beautician in town and has been, mostly, for the last 30 years. There isn't much she doesn't know about what is happening at the moment or that has happened since about 1970. She grew up in Cashtown, PA not far from here and went into the profession of cosmetology after high school. She has been married three times, has children from all the marriages and grandchildren nearly everywhere it seems in a 200 mile radius, and seems perfectly happy with her life as it is now. She speaks wistfully of earlier urges to travel or move on. She and husband one or two, it was hard to tell, lived in Pittsburgh for a time, but she came back "after that was over" as she put it, and seemed to have little reason to feel moving would make her life more interesting or complete. She is happy here by the side of the road caring for the tresses of the ladies of all ages. I never needed to ask whether there were those she did not have as customers, ones who might go over to one of the" big" towns like Mount Holly Springs. She made it clear she didn't care for all the hair on all the heads of the female population of the town, so that was enough. She was an unofficial goodwill ambassador for me at least (it didn't seem like this was the first time she had performed this noble gesture). She told me all I wanted to know about the town and more.

When my father would drive us somewhere on a trip and pass through a town like this one, he often would say that he never could figure out what all the people did for a living since there was nothing obvious that stood out as a means of support. Pennsylvania is famous for small towns with homes built right to the sidewalk with narrow front porches that crowd the street. They were built in a time when the towns were less populated, the traffic on the main street less congested and the people who lived there took the evening breeze and conversations there. It is quite different than the Midwest where a lawn is interposed between the porch and the street and they are more likely found on side streets. Here many are found right along the main streets. Not all these towns had side streets to speak about. Many here are still this way. The porches, some of them, still seem to be used. They have a pair of rocking chairs or a swing and some, even hanging plants. The truly tacky have that green carpet referred to as "indoor/outdoor" for reasons that never made sense to me since I never saw anyone use it indoors. It was clear when you drove through this places that the people had jobs, it was just tough to figure out what they were.

Well, Dot knows what they do for a living in her town. Most people who live here work at the vegetable packing plant. It began as shift work at reasonable wages in good seasons, and they saved for the winter. Trucks come all year now both to take the produce away, but also to bring the raw product from many places. The packing plant was a local concern once, but Dot says it is big business now, packing from two or three states.

I asked her about the Possum Hollow Inn. After a silent moment, Dot shook her head and said that it was usually full of the field hands of little substance and the lower order of packing plant employees on the weeknights. I took this to mean the local former high school types who had not yet, or never would, make a move to leave. She said I could go there if I liked but the food wasn't much and the whiskey wasn't either. The weekends there are the interesting times when the sheriff comes regularly and the pool cues get broken, sometimes over people's heads. Of course, she said, it had been years since she had been there but her customers tell her about such things now and she supposes there is no good reason to go if some fool is just going to crack a pool cue over someone else's head. Especially since the owner can't even buy a decent brand of whiskey. I never did find out what a "decent brand" was to Dot, but it seemed to be important to her.

There are three churches in town, each sounding more like something out of a tale about Lake Wobegon than the last. Lutherans and Episcopalians were the majority, but a fair amount of Baptists are there as well. The ministers were all eccentric, or odd in some way to hear Dot tell it. Not in a bad way, they all just seemed to be odd or strange in one of their manners, habits, dress or speech. They sounded as if they were all older men who had been here a long time and knew a great deal about the people in town. Apparently Dot had been a member of all these ministries over the years so she knew first hand and didn't necessarily have to rely on the chatter of her customers. Once or twice, Dot referred to them as "busybodies." I took that to mean, in the way she said it, that there was a reason why she had changed religions over the years. Dot, I don't believe, much cared for people who knew more about her life than she cared to tell them.

Politics came up in a sly sort of way. There was no real doubt which side of the Christian Coalition she came down on or that "Rush" was a staple of her morning radio listening. I feigned but a passing interest in the subject, opined that all politics are local as Tip O'Neill once said, but didn't attribute the quote. She thought it a fine one, and, I suspect some heard it while having a wash and set sometime later in the week.

I took my leave, having drunk enough tea for several weeks and smelled enough smoke to remember why I quit. Dot said to stop back when I came through again, should I ever do that. I told her I would, and thanked her for all the insight into the town. She said that she had barely scratched the surface but that it was a good place, with good people in it mostly, if you didn't count the young and the stupid and thanked me for sharing the afternoon with her and some of the things about the trip that she declared "amazing." It was a word I had heard a lot from her that day. The vegetable packers were amazing; the church services were sometimes amazing. It seemed a word she liked.

I left with an appreciation of rural small town life I have likely never had before. Some might say that Dot and the others here live lives of quiet desperation, with a cigarette in one hand and a TV remote in the other, listening to the opinions of talk show hosts and adopting them as there own, moving from pay check to pay check, working too many hours for too little money and ruining their health with every puff of smoke, side of beef and bottle of "good whiskey" they consume.

Yet, there is something else. They never lock their doors and it seems that, except for the guys at the Possum, no one much bothers each other unless asked. They take care of each other in times when they need to cry and times when they need to be alone and seem to enjoy each other's company. It makes the world a little less frightening and a little friendlier for them the rest of the time. This small town life is hard for me to make up my mind about. Maybe it isn't bad or good. Or maybe, and more likely, it is not for me to judge.

FOURTEEN

LEBANON AND THE LACKAWANNA VALLEY

I arrived at noon at the home of a friend former co-worker, his lovely wife and his two daughters of 5 and 3. He had a driveway perfect for the first test of such living and, he had built a ramp to his front door. A palace for a prince!

I had a lovely stay. Being in a house and not the van most of the day was more foreign to me than I had expected. The girls got me up to date on all the latest toys, games videos and other matters. It is interesting how those of us who do not live in the constant company of children forget that they really run the house. As we three talked and caught up, beat up politicians and bureaucrats, and excoriated the injustice of the world, there were occasions when the parent "look" would come into their eyes and the conversation would be left dangling while the child was helped, rescued, or answered. Parents do not even know they are doing this and I did not take this as an intrusion into my selfish wish to make my point. It is the way it is with little children about. I was going to see lots of them, so I was learning now what it would be like in other places. The conversation would be picked up, or sometimes a new topic would be introduced once the interrupting child's needs had been met. It was a lovely visit and I began to appreciate how easy it is to live in my efficiency apartment if someone else is cooking dinner or providing lunch. They even let me use the laundry, so I went back out on the road well fed and with clean clothes.

I have been hearing "we need rain" from everyone since Florida. It began Sunday and washed out a patio lunch planned at a local restaurant. I left Monday in a light drizzle that, by the time I went northeast 30 miles, was a downpour. There was no need to complain of a lack of water in the Lackawanna Valley that day. It followed me to Milford on the Delaware Water Gap. It is a place that I have always wanted to visit. Those of us that grew up on the "other" side of New Jersey always believed it to be a lovely and rural place where the river could be enjoyed free of the pollution and chaos of the downstream industrial and boat activity. There may be a lovely river there. I did not see it. Fog or low clouds clung to the hills and made for a very different sort of world. This is the Lackawanna Valley, once very much the industrial heartland of Pennsylvania. Time has been good to it economically, better than Lebanon, where the plant closed in 1973 and everyone still talks about it as if it was yesterday and it will open again soon and solve all the problems. These towns near Scranton; Old Forge, Dickson City, Moosic and others have been, until recently, pretty well supported by various industries. At one stop, I talked to some plant workers from Big Bill's, which had made television parts here for years and been good to the people who worked for them. That is changing. The company is taking advantage of NAFTA and moving the plant and the jobs to Mexico. Many of the workers will qualify for assistance to start new careers, funded by NAFTA provisions that few knew about until this happened. They all freely admit that when the news got around that the plant was leaving, they were angry because they thought their loyalty to the company should mean something. Few knew that retraining opportunities were possible or provided to them if they qualified. These people now have the opportunity to become Physician Assistants and receive other occupational training. Some even admit to being happy about it since the opportunities will be greater than if they worked 30 years in the plant. There are bitter people, of course, but a surprising number accept the fact that the manufacturer had to do what it had to do. The Lackawanna Valley may be dying, the manufacturing base gone just as the plants and the mines in other parts of this hauntingly beautiful land of Victorian homes and Church steeple towns. It is hard to accept that a place so beautiful can be without opportunities. It is also hard for these people who, when asked to tell you what the area will be like, or even where they will be in the next few years, can't since they have no real plan. This was not the last time I saw this attitude in this unique industrial "rust belt" state. It was disturbing. There is much beauty here, but not much opportunity.

I saw the lovely low clouds and mist that shrouded the green hills as I drove on to Medford at the New York border. There was drizzle in the campsite that evening. Many of us were just coming off the road for the night, although my neighbor had been there for a few days. He told me that the site was very nice in summer, with rafting and fishing, although that part of the site was closed off for two more weeks until Memorial Day. The owners are expecting a full house then. The place wasn't exactly as advertised, since the store and office had burned down two weeks before, but that wasn't much of an issue once the rain started to get heavy. I am sure it is a lot bigger issue for the owners with the peak season on the way. It rained hard by early morning. The sound on the roof was pleasant. I had only taken electricity on board the night before since I knew getting to and undoing the hook ups in my tree shaded, dirt campsite would be torture in the morning if it were raining. I was right. I was, at one critical juncture, slipping sideways down the hill while holding firmly to the rear bumper of the van with one hand, and unhooking the electrical cord with the other. It would have made an interesting picture. I completed the task and got the cord stowed and myself back inside, and was full of self-congratulatory pride at having the good sense to have only the one thing to disengage in the rain. I took pride in my prescient behavior. I had a smugness about how well I do this that kept me pleased with myself for the remainder of the morning.

A meal seemed like the thing to do since the run from here to the Baseball Hall of Fame was going to be an all day trip. I found a crowded restaurant in early afternoon with precious few handicapped parking spaces. It occurred to me at one point that I should park in the back with the bigger rigs, but decided to be pushy and used what I thought was a space and a half so that I could deploy the lift. I or anyone else do not recommend this. The van has a sign on the side asking folks not to park within a certain distance and when I got out it appeared to me that there was not a chance anyone would see the spot I was blocking, much less use it, since the van hid it pretty well. That rationalization led to a longer stay than I had planned.

I ate well, and, when ready to leave found a car, a Toyota to be exact, had somehow managed to wedge itself in the space. I could find no visible handicapped designation on it, but since I was ignorant of how they are designated in Pennsylvania, I wasn't sure. I could not lower the ramp, so to wait was my only choice. I went back in the restaurant and the owner eyed me in an odd way. I explained that I was blocked in and would have to wait. She said she would try to find out who owned it and see if they would move the car. I suggested it was my fault and was in no hurry, but she did her civic duty anyway. Since she ran a restaurant with no proper van accessible spaces, I decided to let her have something to do.

Apparently, she found the owner of the car sitting near where I had been just a few minutes before who told her he would move it when he was finished eating. There was a family that had been there when I was one table away who, on their way out, expressed their amazement at the fellow's stupidity and asked if they could move it for me. The lot was tight and the seat in the van was set up on the swivel platform for me to enter the side so I said thanks, but I would wait. The man said," you think maybe three minutes out of his life would be too much, huh?" I agreed, and then was told by another departing couple that they were sorry, and that the man and his wife were actually arguing about it while they ate. I thought that a rather sad commentary.

The rain had slackened so I went out to look at the car and wait. I found that on the dashboard there was what appeared to be a very old "temporary disability" permit and, on the license plate holder, the name of the local volunteer Fire Department. Now I decided the guy was a jerk, not a disabled jerk, just a jerk. He eventually emerged with his wife. He was, to be kind, morbidly obese. She was a sweet looking old woman who looked like she would rather be somewhere else. He waddled into his car somehow managing to get in the driver's door, which was very close to the van. We never spoke. He never looked at me. Because the van hid the oncoming traffic, he had to crawl slowly out of the space while I sat at the rear of the van and watched, offering no help. He left the lot hurriedly. I called the Fire Department when I was reunited with my telephone in the van and gave them the license number and in summary, told them that it was unfortunate such individuals were the best they could do for volunteers in their department and that I was sure that he had not acted as a goodwill ambassador for them this day. In fact, the irony was that he likely annoyed more people in the restaurant than me with his reasonably dumb behavior. They didn't disagree and I went off into the gathering afternoon mist a bit wiser.

FIFTEEN

COOPERSTOWN, GLIMMERGLASS, AND A PLACE CALLED ROTTERDAM

I stayed on the Interstate Highway entering New York State at Port Jervis. The rain followed me as I began my pilgrimage to the Baseball Hall of Fame at Cooperstown. These were not great roads, even for Interstates. However, the farm country they pass through is lovely. One could easily fantasize snuggling down in front of a fire in one of the many old farmhouses nestled in the hills. The towns are small, lived in and lovely. I am only sorry I could not have taken the more scenic route to see more of them. There are not many roads up this way that will take you through the towns, fewer remnants of U.S. highways that are as prevalent in so many other places. The Interstate follows their old roadbeds, and going through town is a great deal out of my way on a rainy day when getting out and looking around isn't likely to be something I want to do.

The town where the Hall of Fame Of Baseball resides is small and, for those of you who have never seen it, the "Hall" sits in the middle of downtown Cooperstown where angle parking is the rule, and no room for handicapped spaces (save four) seems to have been made. There have been moves to move the Hall elsewhere on many occasions. They have all failed, since the type of baseball Abner Doubleday invented is connected in some way to Cooperstown. It may or may not be true that his version is the one true beginning. It is clear now that there were a number of games being played in the United States before the Civil War that involved a bat and a ball and could have served as the wellspring of the modern game. On my way here, I noticed that the Soccer Hall of Fame is now ensconced in an equally small village. This new addition may be why the talk of moving the mementoes of "America's Game" to New York City or somewhere more accessible to the people have subsided of late. There is something to be said for this remoteness. It requires a pilgrimage to come here and you have to want to since getting to this part of the state is not all that easy from, say, San Francisco. I wondered as I rolled into town this day how they manage to get all those people here for the Induction Ceremony every year. The players who come to greet the new inductees are hardly youngsters, and many of the inductees aren't either. I suppose there are a lot of limousine rentals that week in Albany and Syracuse.

I had not made plans to go to the Hall the day I arrived. That was just as well since downtown was full and it was raining, which was enough to discourage me from hunting for fringe parking and finding my way back to the Cathedral of Baseball. I thought I might have a better chance at parking somewhere near it, or finding someone who knew where more parking was in the morning. Cooperstown is quaint in its way, although a bit overrun by souvenir shops and bars and restaurants all with cute, baseball related names like "The Dugout" (it was in a basement). So I went on to find the "Glimmering Glass" state park campsite.

The Hudson River author, Washington Irving, who wrote "Leatherstockings", gave Lake Otsego that name in his book. It borders the town and, I am sure, when it is not a fog bank, it is lovely. The campsite is eight miles from town, on the other side of the lake. The signs through town are clear, but the directions, as in the case of many of the state campsites it seems, become less clear the closer you get. I expect they assume local knowledge, or that you would be smart enough to stop and ask someone. The distances in the directions in my travel guide seemed to be wrong, which was unusual for the source book I have been using. The road is very narrow and closely borders the other side of the lake. It has those signs we all see and ignore about "Watch for Fallen Rock". Well folks, I am here to tell you they do fall, particularly in the rain. They land in the road. They get run over it and do real damage. I know that as a certain fact. I did it.

The Van continued to run fine after the encounter, but the sewage release pipe and holding tank valves were mangled beyond reason. There are, of course, no RV repair places in or near Cooperstown, nor did my cell phone work there. Lastly, the shoulders on the road are too narrow to use safely so, until I actually found the Park, I had to simply imagine what all that noise was when the rocks bounced up and hit the undercarriage.

The rain was not letting up. A cursory inspection told me that I had serious damage that needed repair but that the van would continue to run fine. Plastic pipe was all that seemed to be broken from what I could see without actually getting out of the wheelchair and laying on the wet ground. Since I knew it was not going to be something I could fix, that seemed extreme. I figured this all out on the cement drive near the Ranger's office. Given my location and the fact that it was now after four o'clock, getting dark, and still raining, it seemed best to stay the night and deal with it in the morning. It all seemed to be staying attached to the van. What looked like it might not I affixed with my handy roll of duct tape. Everyone knows that the stuff will hold almost anything together at the speed of sound if necessary for at least a week. I decided I could make it through the night since everything else was working so far as I could tell. I needed a plan, but I didn't need it until morning. My respirations were back to normal now, so I decided that, since the rain was picking up again, that it would have to wait until then.

I went into the office and learned from the semi-friendly ranger that I would have to avoid two campsites, which were in use, but as far as she was concerned, any of the other 150 sites were fine since they were unoccupied. She seemed mildly interested in my woes when I asked if there were any repair facilities in the area, but said she didn't think so and mumbled something about Albany, so I let it go at that.

It is a self-contained park, which means no electric except what you have aboard. The generator helps in times like these. It was cold, it poured most of the evening and I was in bed not long after dark wondering what would be next. Given the correct state of mind and reasonable weather, it would be quite lovely here. My next stop was due to be the Boston area and my niece's driveway, so the repairs had to be made somewhere. I spent a cold gray evening, perhaps the only lonely one of the trip, trying to make a plan.

It is odd how I felt that all the support systems I had in place had failed all at once. I had no power. I had no telephone. I was sufficiently off the beaten path to not be able to find an RV repair place. Yet, I had food, I had heat and a generator for lights and I was dry. Priorities change in these situations. I was not in any danger, and yet, my compulsive personality screamed for a solution to the problem beyond such homilies as "God will provide." I wanted to know what I would do and where I would go in the morning to fix this and go on. I did not want to have to figure it all out. I wanted to call or ask someone what to do next and have him or her tell me. Instead, I felt confused and unable to formulate a plan. I was not pleased with what I now thought was just one more flaw in my character. Yet the answers would not come. As it got darker, I convinced myself that it would all be clearer in the morning. I slept fitfully, secure only in the knowledge that the van would start in the morning, I could then get back to a place where the telephones worked and talk to my friends in Canada at the van company who, I hoped, would have a solution for me. If I had a plan, that was it. The day had been a long one. It probably contributed to my sour mood and inability to focus. I went to bed early and read in an eerily quiet and nearly empty campground.

-2-

In the morning it was still as gloomy. There were two more campers in the site this morning, no doubt late arrivals. I got the van ready to move, thus forfeiting my second night here, but not really feeling like stopping at the office to explain it all just to recover the fee. By about 8 AM I was out of the site and stopped at the waste dump to see if anything was going to work. It was pouring when I pulled into it. The good news about these dumpsites is that most are on cement pads, which make them easy to move around on. I hooked up and managed to release most of the wastewater. It did not go through the pipe but dropped on the sluice of cement just behind it. The good news, was that I noted that the "grey water" tank was intact and the valve worked. I was not as sure about the "black water" tank, which would be very bad news. I cleaned it up by washing it all down with the hose provided at these places and began my trip out.

I passed through Cooperstown. The Hall was already busy and for a moment I regretted that I would not see it this trip. I rationalized it all by reminding myself that the place is so big now that it takes two or more days to see it all and that I had seen films of it. I still remembered the considerably smaller place my father and brother had come to visit the mementos of Ruth, Gehrig, Cy Young, and many others. I have not seen the actual place in perhaps 45 years, so there is certainly much more there now. That makes seeing it a more daunting a task. The rain was not letting up; I did stop for a few minutes to look around the main lobby. It makes some luxury hotels look like fleabags. I left shortly and I went on to try to solve my own problems and to continue the trip.

Being on a solo flight added to my melancholy. I most certainly did not want to spend the Memorial Day weekend in a motel by the side of the road. Yet, I had two days to fix the van and get to Massachusetts. I felt pressured and I did not like the feeling. I wanted to spend the long weekend with family and I also knew that RV repair people would be especially busy right now, three days before the weekend. Other than knowing I had at least two hours before I would be able to talk to the factory because of the time difference, I had only a vague idea what I would do next. I left rural New York for Interstate 88 and headed towards Albany in the belief that if there was help, it would likely be there.

-3-

Rotterdam, NY was not a town I chose. But then, many of the places I have been were not. It is, as someone said, "just part of the trip." For a reason that is only clear to my personal god and serendipity, I got off Interstate 88 here and found a lot of very nice people.

As I approached the Rotterdam exit, I realized in one of those moments of blinding reality, that I was about to pay a toll and be hermetically sealed on the New York Thruway. I needed fuel and was desperately to eat something since my cold breakfast was wearing thin. For all these not very essential reasons, I took the famous "last exit before toll" having no real idea where I was. I was delighted to find a gas station and a Dunkin' Donuts Shop right next to each other. That, and the fact that the day was brightening despite the continued drizzle, was almost heaven itself. It was also approaching the hour when I could call the manufacturer and see if he could find a dealer for me somewhere nearby.

After fueling the van and me, I asked a nice lady behind the counter if she knew anyone who might be able to at least crawl under my van and tell me how bad things really were before I continued. She, startlingly, took an immediate interest and said, why sure, she would call her mechanic who was five miles down the road and ask him. She did and he said he would look when I got there. He also admitted he had no idea how to fix the mess he saw and knew very little about "these RVs", but he knew that Jack White at the RV place a few more miles in the other direction would be able to check it.

White's RV Repair turned out to be a very large hangar-like structure at the end of a very muddy road. Jack himself wandered out after a time (since my getting out was not going to be an option) and said he was just finishing one and would look at mine in about ten minutes. This seemed luck enough, since at least I would know whether anything was falling off or just how extensive a delay I might be facing. He looked. He groaned, but he thought he could fix it. He searched for parts and started to pull it apart. It turned out there was a part peculiar to my van that he didn't have and could not find in the parts books. I knew this was not good news, but he seemed to know what he was talking about, which was encouraging. I called Leisure Van in Canada and talked to the service manager. Jack then talked to him about what he needed and he said he had the parts and would express them overnight. That would get the parts here the next day and Jack said he could install them. Now all I needed was a place to live until they could fix it. Jack and his helper gave me some motel names and on the first call a lady named Debbie at the Rotterdam Inn found space for me for the 23rd and 24th and could give it to me in the next hour. That was good since it would get me out of the van and indoors. I also had a lot of e-mail to catch up on and the phone was getting reception now, so I was able to let everyone know where I was and when I would likely get to my next destination, if the parts showed up and Jack was as good a mechanic as I hoped.

It was not the motel, from appearances or location that I would have picked out on my own, but Jack proved right when he had said that the people who ran it were "good people" and it was quiet there. The people turned out to be part of the Peloso family that owned the restaurant next store. "Debbie", who was still at the desk when I got there, greeted me warmly and the rest of the desk folks over the next two days could not have been nicer. Everyone felt a little sorry for the Californian stuck here in the rain, I think. I settled in for a wait and tried to stay amused. I caught up on my logs, e-mail, and phone calls and checked the maps for a likely place to stay after I left Jefferson, MA, and despaired that HBO movies were the only ones available and really terrible. I read some of the book that had been sitting on the shelf in the van getting scant attention up until now.

I also had time to reflect on the trip so far. Except for the weekend in Pennsylvania with friends, I had been pretty much on my own. This was the end of a part of the journey where I was truly solo. It seemed, as I thought back on all the places I had been and calculated the miles, that there had been a few disasters, but nothing terrible and it had been an exploration of many interesting small towns and parks and roadside wonders. Most who know me well would not describe me as an explorer in the sense that I enjoy a new place every day or so. I like routines. I like people I recognize. I used to take the same flights and airlines because I got to know the crew. It makes me comfortable. Yet here I was in a hotel in a town I had never been in before, after traveling thousands of miles and staying one and two nights in places I had never been before, having eaten in hundreds of restaurants I had never seen before, content in the knowledge that I had done it and sure from my memories, that I had enjoyed it very much.

The van, which I had owned for three months before the trip, and now driven nearly every day for over a month was a complex vehicle that I seemed to have mastered and was enjoying more than I ever thought I would. Given the opportunity to live in it or a motel, or even someone's house, I chose it. I really was enjoying the experience. Yet I am not thought of as a person who enjoys unknown things. I was rekindling a spirit, it seemed that had died sometime after I left the Navy when the unknown was more fun than anything else in the world. It seemed to me that perhaps this injury, so many years ago, had changed me, and had made me a man more of habits than spontaneity. That once was my middle name, yet, until this trip, it seemed to have changed. Yet I would not feel happy, I knew, until the parts were here and installed and I could move on. I had nieces and nephews, and at last count, nine of their children waiting.

I was sustained by the Italian take-out or eat in place of the Peloso family next door It has the same baker as when Grandfather Peloso came from Italy. Their motto is: "Watch Pizza Made by Imported Hands." The food is fantastic. I would get AAA to give them five stars if I could.

At mid-day on Thursday, I had not heard from my new best friend Jack, so I got in the van and drove over there. He had the parts but was in the midst of an emergency repair on a huge "fifth wheel" trailer that was likely worth more than my house. A motor home is known as a fifth wheeler when it is attached to its tow vehicle much as a trailer on a big truck. It is a trailer and there is a mount in the floor over the axle of what is an oversized pickup truck. The trailers can be 40 feet long and have sides that slide out so that the square footage when fully deployed is enormous. Many people prefer them because you can unhitch the truck. There are motor coaches that approximate the size of a bus that have the same sliding walls and achieve at least the same interior space, but a car must be towed behind since they are not something you can park easily on the main street of town. If you see a large pick up truck with what looks like a split rail fence for a tailgate and a large bump in the middle of the truck bed, you are looking at a truck that tows a fifth wheeler. Jack said he would be a couple of hours so I said I would get something to eat and come back around three.

I went back down the street to the truck stop and observed the many over the road truckers who were pulling in at this hour for a hot meal.

These men and women keep strange hours. By dinnertime for the rest of the world, they will be off the road resting for the night ahead. They eat either an early dinner or a late lunch, depending on your point of view and will eat again later as they drive on into the night while you sleep. It is hard to tell from the food, since they are just as likely to eat a steak now as at ten tonight. None want to participate in the quaint ritual of rush hour, so they eat now and then rest while the rest of the world is in the bumper to bumper maze fighting their way home. Then they will drive well into the night, as far as their logbooks and the inspectors will allow. 12 hours a day behind the wheel is not uncommon, but it usually comes with rest stops and sleep in between. There are the crazy ones, and the good ones will tell you about them, who push a load as fast as they can and then catch a load headed back where they came from. They do caffeine, cigarettes, and whatever drugs it takes. Most don't work that way and many now drive in family pairs. There are a few lone woman drivers out here, but still not many, and they have to have skin as thick as an elephant to take the remarks they catch from the males, who see their domain being violated. Political Correctness has yet to invade the cabs of big rig trucks.

The large, over the road vehicles that are privately owned have cabs that are longer than my van now and the back of them look like condos. They have everything I have in mine and can cost more than an oversized motor home. Yet somehow they haul enough to make the payments, and the size of these things in recent years have made it possible for the family run rigs to become more plentiful simply because they are more comfortable. When I was young, I remember a real luxury model of the time as having a shelf behind the seat that was a bed where one driver slept as they took turns at the wheel to achieve the maximum distances. Now, husbands and wives team up to be out on the road for six or more months at a time.

When I was finished eating and watching, I went back and waited while Jack found more trouble with the big rig than he had hoped. He started on mine about 6 PM and it took about two hours, but he fixed it. I was beginning to feel much better. While he was wandering around (he had a habit of forgetting where he put a tool down) putting me back together as it were, I learned he only did this part time for now, had only been in this building for a short time and was, in real life, a cop in Schenectady and was planning on taking an early retirement next year and do this full time. I was sure he would do well. He had that way with people that allowed him to hear you but not get too involved and to thank you while turning down things offered without offending. My latest new friend Fred, the owner of the fifth wheeler, had pulled out, plugged into the power of the building and was making dinner (or "the wife" was). He had come back to introduce himself and apologize for how long it had taken to get fixed up and he offered us some of the stew being cooked in his palace as we spoke. Jack declined on the grounds that his wife had brought him a sandwich, and I did on the grounds that I had already eaten. It was amazing, I remember thinking, that these huge rigs, which are truly houses on wheels, could sit in a muddy field full of repaired, wrecked and rusted RVs and never really know the difference.

My van was declared well at about 8:30 PM and I was effusive in my thanks to Jack and I headed back to the hotel. It was dark when I got in, but one more trip to the Peloso's restaurant netted me stuffed shells as good as I have had in a long while. One shower later, I was in bed and ready for my trip to Massachusetts the next day, as content as I had been since I had left Pennsylvania.

Once again, it had been necessary to rely on the random acts of kindness of strangers. And once again I had been handsomely rewarded. For all of my angst over this stop I enjoyed myself and met some people I would not have and certainly ate and slept well. Reward is sometimes wrapped in strange paper.

SIXTEEN

MEMORIAL DAY, JEFFERSON, MASSACHUSETTS

After the long evening of repair work in Rotterdam, the ride to my nieces house outside of Worcester should have been anticlimactic. It would have been completely without comment if I had copied the directions correctly. Instead, I missed a critical turn and I saw a little more of Massachusetts than I had planned. I arrived at about 2 PM on Friday to a lovely home full of people I either had not seen in a very long time, or never had met at all. Two of the children have been born and the rest have been busy growing up since I had last been to the East Coast. Ones that were toddlers the last time I saw them are now teenagers, or nearly so. There was much catching up to do. It is interesting how family members are familiar even when it has been nearly a decade since your last encounter. We have all changed, but we have all stayed the same.

There were no parades. I am sure that one could have found Memorial Day things if one was interested, but we did not do more than fly the flag. An early morning radio show did afford me with the origin of "Taps" which; given my previous professions and my recent trip to Gettysburg gave it a special meaning. I remember its' lonesome sound well from Boot Camp. It was the haunting melody that lulled me to sleep every night before it had finished. I remember it from the parades we had every year in the town where I grew up. There is a way to play it with two buglers that makes one sound like the echo of the other. I had never known where the tune had come from.

The name derives from the time of the Civil War when, at evening during battle, three "taps" on the drum meant no talking and all lights out. General James Butterfield wrote the current version, which is short, but longer than the drum taps and it was played on the bugle in the evening and continued to signify the end of the day. Like so many things that were a remembrance of a time or place for a soldier, it began to be used at funerals to signify the final quiet that a soldier knows. It was used unofficially and sporadically at funerals during the latter part of the Civil War. Like the singing of "Danny Boy" at an Irishman's funeral, or playing bagpipes. It officially became part of the funeral ceremonies for a fallen soldier in 1891. It was good to learn all that on such a special day.

The weather was alternately lovely and abysmal, but not bad enough now that I have had all this practice with rain again to matter to me. I am losing my California aversion to wet weather. There was a very large track meet in which the oldest of my great nieces had a large part, 200 meters and the 4x200 relay. The meet was Saturday and, the day dawned as if it would rain and we went to the meet quite prepared for it. However, sunscreen was necessary before the end of the first hour. I had forgotten how long it takes to run a track meet. It is like going to the racetrack. One waits a very long time between the events. Then they are over in but an instant of time and a fury of energy on the part of the competitors. My great niece set records in her event and it was lovely to see someone who truly knows how to run a race and not just get around the track. Since five adults and six of the siblings of two of my nieces were there, it was hardly dull. While less than a few minutes were needed to appreciate my great niece's efforts, the rest of the day was spent visiting among ourselves. By early afternoon we were looking for shade. As is the way of these things, both for the competitor's sake and organization, all the sprints were run early and all the relay events were run late. Since many of the sprinters are also part of the relay teams it can't be done any other way. However, if you are there merely to watch one person, and know absolutely no one else involved in the races in between, it can seem a bit like an eternity before they get to it.

The next day brought more rain. I decided a muddy soccer field was not where I wanted to be so stayed at the house and was alternatively charmed and amusingly terrorized by the youngest family members. The game I missed was bizarre. The referee disqualified two of the other teams' goalies shortly after the beginning of the second period. All that went to the game said they could not remember seeing, nor had heard of a goalie even being warned, much less ejected from a game. With the visiting team now goalie-less, the opposing coach took the team off the field and forfeited the game under the prevailing theory of most who attended that the referee was a sandwich shy of a picnic and to use a non-goalie person at that point would likely be asking someone to get hurt .

The next day began clear and cool and my niece's husband Matthew gave a demonstration of slalom on a riding tractor, aided a bit later by the second, Bill, who is a rather large man once an anchor in the Holy Cross College offensive line. He has been described as a building with clothes on. He nearly did "wheelie" at the start of his turn around the acreage. Matt also had about 5 yards of mulch he was determined to get spread that day so Bill and I did a reasonably accurate imitation of Department of Public Works employees by leaning on shovels while Matt raced around the yard with a wheelbarrow full of mulch. We would fill it, he would go somewhere to dump and spread it and we would hang out. Folks actually do this for a living, and Bill and I computed that, with holiday overtime, we would have made a great deal of money had we been employed by the city or the state. We were content to visit. After all, lunch was provided when yet another shower arrived in the late afternoon.

The population of the household is sufficiently diverse in age that people sort of come and go, as they need to participate in events and visit with friends. Visiting Bill is about as rabid a member of the Red Sox Nation as possible. He is quickly indoctrinating his two sons. When not otherwise occupied, he would sit in the living room demanding that someone turn on the game. He alone seemed to know the time schedule for these things.

The television was equipped with a "game boy" device. I confessed at some point that in all the years of their existence and all the years of mine, I had never actually tried to play a game on it. Patrick, the 14 year old of the house who was for the past few days hobbled by an injury to his leg from a soccer game and enjoying it not all, offered to show me the mysteries of the game boy world. We started with basketball, which seemed simple enough. I managed, because I still believe Patrick was tanking the game, to keep it close. I beat him at the buzzer with a three point shot. He was not pleased since I think he expected to play it close but prevail in the end. I then began relating to anyone who would listen how I had beaten the stuffing out of him, which pleased him less. It was actually an interesting lesson, the coordinative movements of ones fingers clearly gives the advantage to the young and dexterous. I am now no longer surprised that professional athletes are usually very adept at the games, and I am told play all the time. After all, they are mostly children anyway, at least in my world, and if not dexterous, would not be making millions doing what they do.

It was a wonderful visit and a time to be cherished by the traveler who will not soon get back this way again to enjoy such good company and food. It was surely a wonderful way to spend a holiday weekend for me, away from the maddening crowds, whatever the weather. I am sure my nieces and their children would have preferred the beach. In the morning they would all be back to school and work, and I would be back on the road. The efficiency of having the van once again prove invaluable when your relatives have a flat driveway and no one is sure of how accessible the house is for a person in a wheelchair. No packing, no moving in and out, and no need to disturb the basic rhythms of life in the household. It also helps that when they get tired, either of listening or because of trials of their day, they can get you down a few steps, into the driveway and not have to deal with you until whatever time they decide is breakfast.

I enjoyed the visit immensely and pulled out as all were returning to their normal life on the morning following the holiday. It was great fun and a wonderful time to renew my memories of all these relatives. There are more to come as the trip goes on and I hope all are as memorable as this one.

SEVENTEEN

CONNECTICUT BY THE SEA

The holiday was over. The traffic had disappeared. I fueled at Sturbridge where I got off the Massachusetts Turnpike and headed down a Scenic Route on Connecticut 169 south that took me through "old" Connecticut. It was a pleasant drive through small towns like Woodstock, Pomfret, Lisbon, and Cantebury with Preparatory Schools and very old homes. The weather was beautiful again, washed clean by the rains. The route was equally lovely. Again, I am struck by how green and lush everything is. I watched the Prep School inhabitants in their blazers move across the road from one very old and lovely building to another between classes this spring morning. It is almost time for summer vacation and graduation. One can almost tell the senior groups as they have a certain swagger in their walk.

A short and pleasant drive later, with a stop for lunch in Brooklyn, a lovely town of restored homes and true New England architecture, and then on to the coast. I pass New London where the Electric Boat Company has been building the Navy's submarines about as long as they have had them and Mystic, a charming New England seacoast town, and into East Lyme. It is a nice town just off US 1, The "Boston Post Road." Lyme is also known as Flanders, but was apparently originally Old Lyme. When you try to figure these things out in the eastern United States, particularly in one of the original thirteen colonies, it becomes difficult. Old Lyme was created or "set off" as they say here, in

February of 1665. So it was a while ago. East Lyme actually bounds the larger town on, surprise, the east while Lyme is to the north. The estimate is that people have lived there and called it one thing or another for 4,000 years. The land is attractive for farming and recreation since it is near the mouth of the Connecticut River. I never found out why all these names got invented and I doubt anyone is completely sure of much since the original setting off from Saybrook back in 1665.

I went west into the countryside to a most pleasant campsite with its own lake and fountains. I needed to make some plans and telephone calls to those I expected to see as I moved down the Eastern Seaboard to Washington, D. C., so I spent three days there with fish and wild fowl in abundance. The folks that own it are interesting. They are no strangers to RVs themselves and looked around the country to see what would work best when they bought this place which had, evidently, fallen into disrepair and been repossessed. It is still seasonal, but they hope to change that this year. They are a family, who seem to genuinely enjoy what they do. It rained a bit, but I still had a day to travel around and see some sights and get errands run. I had the heat on one night. I apparently was not alone, although there were few of us in the sites. I was assured at the office that the weekend had been "a zoo", which would be expected since, as I have mentioned, it is still a month until summer, but all easterners believe it starts on Memorial Day.

Since I was there three nights, I got to see a number of comings and goings. The neighborliness of the south has been replaced by a quiet hello, which may have had more to do with how few of us there were and the chilly weather than attitude. I tried to relax before this next section of the trip that was pretty well scripted and people intensive. There were a few people that came through for a night, including one likely certifiable crazy in 30-foot camper from Florida. He and his wife arrived one site over from me. She was driving and he was doing the talking, mostly about the way she was driving. He yelled at her the whole time she was situating the motor coach on the site, appeared to merely accept the final resting place as the best she could do, and then he preceded to check tires and fluids and clean windows and otherwise busy himself about the thing. She was not seen again until 7:30 the next morning when, with her at the wheel again, they pulled out. My speculation was that he likely had some physical condition that had lifted his license and he was less than happy about it. People who suffer a blackout, for example, and seek treatment are reported to the DMV in most states and required to wait a year to drive again. He seemed agitated enough to be one of those, although maybe he just was annoyed with most everything and chose to give her a hard time about it and just chose not to drive.

My refuge from these sideshows was to show up in the office every morning and drink coffee with the "management" and whoever else happened to be around. I doubt that the emptiness of the campgrounds was as pleasant for the owners as it was for me. This visit was a most pleasant way to start the day, where good conversation and even a newspaper could be found. I had not read one in earnest since April that I could remember so the news truly was news to me. The owners talked of becoming, after four years, an all year park instead of only being open for the "season." In campgrounds terms, the season is loosely defined as April to October in most places. It is understandable since they now have people who stay with them until they close and then have to move up or down the road. They would like to keep these loyal customers and garner the ground rent. Closing probably costs money because the rent is lost and the place has to be winterized. There is a part of me that likes the seasonal parks since folks don't tend to move in for good and build porches and tool sheds and such and stay so long they may as well take the wheels off the rigs and put it on blocks. I suppose there is a way to keep that from happening, but I have not yet seen a year 'round park that didn't have a few of these denizens. I think they make it less fun since they tend to "own" the best spaces and seem to clutter the place up.

It is hard to tell what one's impressions are of this state. It is incredibly diverse. The center of the insurance world is in Hartford, many colleges and preparatory schools dot the landscape in the more quiet and inland settings, yet the seacoast is submarine sailors, the Coast Guard Academy, and a base where they do many things, including teach new naval officers to drive ships. This is a part of the "black shoe Navy", those who man the ships and submarines and service them as well. The "brown shoe Navy" are strictly aviators, and to the men and women here, not real Navy at all. The terms come from the fact that, once commissioned, the officers who fly do wear brown shoes with certain uniforms, while the "real" Navy people never do.

The coast is a ragged and rocky one of both the Atlantic Ocean and Long Island Sound. It is Interstate 95 carrying folks headed to Boston and beyond and, except for Herbert Walker Bush and son George, people who grew up here, and a few overpaid New York executives of all industries, who have palatial homes in the southern part of the state, it can be largely lost in the place we know as "New England." It seems a place to pass through for most of us, although, when we stop, we find beauty. The coastal areas are largely areas of working fisherman or, alternately, towns as quaint and lovely as Mystic and many others, most with unpronounceable Indian names.

I enjoyed my stay. I hope the park will flourish and the owners who were so kind to me will as well. It was time now to move on to more family and some friends and to revisit places I had not seen in what seemed like a very long time.

EIGHTEEN

TENAFLY

I left Connecticut early enough to suffer the horrors of Interstate 95 between traffic jams and suffer the construction (it has been and likely always will be under construction) and to leave time to visit Tenafly, New Jersey, the place where I, at least physically, grew up.

Shortly before I was born, my father moved the family to this bucolic setting in Northern New Jersey from New York City. All of his family remained on the "civilized" side of the Hudson River. He had only sisters, and I believe most of them were not sure whether there were Indians on the New Jersey side, but stayed there as a matter of both practicality and principle. They were New Yorkers, after all, and the Hudson River was "The River", the demarcation between civilization and the rest of the United States.

We moved to a small house in what would now be known as a tract. The community was one of the first "bedroom" towns for commuters to New York. Most of the men got on the train every morning and rode down the valley to the place where it connected with the mass transit systems of New York. My Father traveled by car and, later, plane all over the east coast so he had no reason; except for the two weeks a year he had to work there, to spend time in "the City." He worked for a company that made carburetors, and, during the war the made a lot of them for military trucks and jeeps. He was exempt because he worked in a defense related industry, although he volunteered to go to war, he was never let in due to some doctor's belief that he had some non existent physical impairment. His willingness to go is well documented in surviving correspondence with his cousin who was a Congressman at the time. As hard as he tried, none of the services would relent, so he stayed deferred.

When the War was over, we moved to the other side of town to a three-story house, which I was sure was the largest house ever built. I was four, which explains the perspective. We moved for many reasons, but mainly because defense contractors made a lot of money, as they do in every war, and my brother was born, which made the present house too small.

When I last saw the house in the early 1990's it was still every bit the stately English Tudor with large trees and a quiet, if worn grace. What I beheld now was a place where the trees and shrubs of a size that hid its massive exterior were now stripped. No replacements had been planted. No other landscaping plan appeared evident. It made the place look naked. It still had a sweeping front lawn atop a six-foot hand built stone wall, but none of the tall trees or shrubs that hid its massive street front exterior. The house sat alone atop the hill. With all the "new" white vinyl "replacement" windows and other higgly piggly renovations done since my last visit, it now is an odd structure with an architectural style that is hard to identify when viewed from the street. It is shabby in appearance, and not a "stately shabby" by any means. It was a sad sight. My mind's eye remembers something much grander. It was I am sure, never as grand as I remembered, but surely grander than this.

This house held so many memories, many good and some very bad. It had been the gathering place for aunts and uncles and grandmothers and great uncles for important holidays. My mother routinely put 25 plates on the table every Thanksgiving and Christmas for more years than I can remember. It was the gathering place for the Burns clan, my Mother's unmarried sisters and would include one or both of her married brothers as well. It was the house where my father died, and the place where my sister, brother and I lived until we went to college and beyond. I was disappointed that it did not remain as a monument to those times.

This was a town I knew intimately. I cannot think of a street in it I had not been. I had friends that lived on them, and had gone to parties on others. I knew them from my short stint as a volunteer fireman. I also likely started a car with a dead battery on most of them on a cold snowy December morning while I worked at the local gas station in high school and on college vacations. I had always, because of this familiarity, thought of it as "my" town, not just the place I grew up.

The residential streets look pretty much the same. There are no empty lots anymore, but that is understandable and what has been built has been generally tasteful. At the top of the East Hill, there had been nothing but something approaching a forest when we first moved there. The really expensive homes have replaced nearly all of that, but that had begun before I had moved out. There were, because of the proximity to New York City, a number of celebrities that at times owned homes there when I was a teen, A number of Yankee ballplayers lived there since it was a quick commute across the George Washington Bridge into the Bronx. Paul Anka, the singer and songwriter lived there for a time when he was a teen idol, and a number of Broadway's stars of the time.

In the downtown area there are many landmarks that have gone missing or turned into new, sometimes unrecognizable things. The place we hung out as teenagers is now a bank. It seems a bit strange since it was a Dairy Queen. The parking lot that every teenager with a car drove into at least once every Saturday night while I was a high school student still surrounds it. Such comings and goings could still be possible, I suppose. We never did go for the ice cream. The town seems much busier now. Boutiques by the dozens, specialty stores and other signs of modern life make up most of the place. Gone is the apothecary, the " Cigar Store" on the corner is now much more than that, and the grocer on Main Street has long disappeared. Even the one chain store we had when I lived there is gone. We thought it a marvel, that old A&P Store. It had its own parking and everything. Across the railroad tracks there is now another of the many non-descript chains food stores as the anchor of a small and tawdry strip mall. It serves the purpose I guess, but the charm is gone.

There remains a wonderful and enormous park—known as the "Common"—which is nearly in the middle of town that has been improved a great deal over the years. It likely gets more use now than it did when my high school was located adjacent to it. That is a "middle" school now. It appears the same, but for the parking lot. We used to park there when we were old enough to drive—a true badge of honor. Given the age of middle school children, I presume they do not drive and yet the parking lot is now twice as big as when it was a high school. I keep wondering if there is something I missed, unless the teacher population has grown exponentially.

Up the street were the athletic fields. There have been many changes. The former varsity baseball diamond has disappeared. It was distinguishable from the junior varsity diamond, shared with the local town 13 year old and above leagues, by the fact that it actually had a grass infield while the other was hard packed dirt, or sand, depending on the time of year since it was never watered. Playing on either was a challenge. The surface of the infield was horrible. As a second baseman I took that seriously. On the Varsity Field a cinder running track crossed the field about twenty feet behind the infield and the outfield consisted of the football field. The track came into play more on the left side of the field than the right as I recall and made leaving the infield for a short fly ball an adventure. Track Meets often occurred the same day as a game, which meant we would have to pause if the event used the full one-quarter mile oval. Some of the baseball team members also were on the track team, so we would leave the bench and participate in our event and return. I ran many a 100-yard dash in running shorts worn under my flannel uniform after shedding the shirt and pants and changing my shoes. The Track and Baseball coaches had to coordinate all this so that we were not on the field but at bat when all this happened. I am not sure how they did that, but I recall that a whistle was involved. The general rule was that baseball took precedence over track, so they might hold up an event while we finished the bottom of an inning, or run an event out of order to accommodate us.

Exercise equipment and a composite track have replaced the varsity field. The junior varsity field is now a real stadium for the little league. The old field house where we dressed for every sport, and which always smelled of some ghastly lineament we were sure would make our throwing arms stronger or our aim truer is now a garage for the Department of Public Works' trucks, lawn mowers and other implements of destruction. Another field house is adjacent to it but it seems too new to have the charm of the old one where the only two showers had some hot water about twice a week.

There was a very small house on a very large lot across the street from the field and the track when I grew up where Edie Adams' mother lived. Edie was an actress and singer on Broadway of some renown, but known best for marrying the comedian of long ago, Ernie Kovacs. He was, for you much younger than I am, the host of the first comedic Late Show on a New York network affiliate that may or may not have been shown elsewhere in the country. It was the precursor of the Tonight Show hosted by so many others and invented by a man named Fritz Weaver.

Ernie came to town occasionally and we would see him. There are stories from those times when Ernie would come to pick up Edie driving his signature white Cadillac. He gave hitchhiking teenagers a ride often and they would watch in awe as he smoked the largest cigar any of us had ever seen. It was his trademark. He was seldom without it while on stage and apparently while he drove to Tenafly to get his wife from the home of his mother-in-law. Now, the house is gone, and one appropriate to the size of the lot has replaced it.

The downtown area has changed little in shape. It is still a T shape of Washington and Railroad Avenues. The commuter train tracks ran along the top of the "T". No one ever seemed to want to make it much larger than that. The two streets that run parallel to the perpendicular of the "T" have filled out a good bit as the town has become less of a self-contained shopping area and more a boutique and specialty store Mecca. But the business district still ends just over the railroad tracks. A storefront or two are familiar, even the names. But most are gone. Significant to the men of my father's generation, the "Office" is gone. It was a bar named by the men who patronized it so they could call home and tell "the wife" they were "still at the office." It was probably funny after a few beers in the 1950's. It is a nail salon now. My father and many of his cronies who had a hand in its naming and spent more time there than they would ever admit, no doubt spun in their graves for a while when that transition took place.

So, after visits to schools where few honors were won, but times were good, and to athletic fields where one failed to meet standards set by others, and did not have the sense to set one's own, and to the houses and places cherished in youth, I left.

I was glad I went. I will not be saddened if I do not go back. I reconciled as many memories with reality as I could. The good that came from it all remains firmly planted in me. The roots are deep and in the right places, despite the frivolity of youth. It is still a lovely town. Perhaps however, for the first time on what may be my last visit, I do not know it as "my" town. It remains the town in my memory where I grew and stayed until I was seventeen and shared the heartaches and the joys that come with attaining that age. I continued to visit there until my Mother's death at 90 in 1991. Many things happened there, which changed my life and that of my family. Yet I don't feel connected to it now. That seems sad somehow. My parents lived there a very long time.

We once possessed the Post Office Box numbered 12 and my mother had the same telephone number in 1943 as she did when she died. There was permanence about all that and it is gone. There is no connection for me. It is perhaps for that reason that the pictures in my mind remain more vivid than the scenes I saw there now. It was a good place to be in the 1950's, ten miles from Greenwich Village and the rest of the "City", which could be visited for a quarter on the bus and a dime on the subway. It was and still is a quiet town with little crime, a volunteer Fire Department and an ambiance that anyone would have enjoyed when they were growing up had they the sense to understand why they had it so good.

I have been harsh perhaps in my criticism of its' change. The problem, I know, is not so much that it has changed, but that we both have, and I was not there to change with it. There are times when you see an old friend and while the greetings are jovial and well meant there is soon a distance between you. It is as if there is little to talk about, little in common. It seems you are both waiting for the other to leave so that you each can be put back in your proper historical perspective. Neither of you remembers the other with gray hair or no hair at all. You have a definite place in a lifetime memory, and now you are here, out of place and it is disorienting.

My trip to Tenafly was a bit like that. It is of course a special place in my memory, but it is not special to me now. Finding fault with it comes easy, but it so resembles what it was like when I lived there it still has meaning and substance. It cannot be reconciled, I know, but it is somehow painful to see a place where I knew nearly everyone and now know nearly no one. I leave, however, in peace. It may be my last visit, but I did enjoy it.

NINETEEN

POINT PLEASANT

My next stop was to see my sister and her husband at their house at the Beach. It turned out, despite the weather, to be the proper antidote for my excursion through Tenafly.

I met them at their house up north and we drove south to the New Jersey shore It was pouring rain again. Ah, the east coast is a wondrous place. My van now smells like a raincoat left hanging for too long on a back porch in Seattle.

They have a house in Point Pleasant Beach. My sister is the only member of my family who remained in New Jersey. They have had this house on the shore since at least 1974, and even through I lived on the East Coast many of those years after the Navy and my rehabilitation, I had never seen it. That does not speak ill of my relationship with my sister. I was a regular visitor to their home in northern New Jersey. There was always a reason why I never got to the "shore house." It was summer. I had a home in a beach community in Delaware called Bethany Beach many of the same summers that they spent at theirs in New Jersey. I had a wheelchair accessible house. I was never sure how accessible the beach house at Point Pleasant was, so one reason I never got there was that if it wasn't, I would have had to drive home again the same day since the chances of finding a motel in that neighborhood on a moments notice in summer would have been slim. Since I had my own beach in the summer, it did not make as much sense to visit there as it did the house in the north where the visit could be combined with one with my Mother.

There were always these and other reasons—I cannot recall that any of the others were good ones either—why I never could find the time to get there.

An interesting regionalism in speech here is that when one goes near the ocean, as I did in my youth and my sister and her husband continue to do in New Jersey, it is to the "shore." When you go to the same place and live in Washington D.C. one goes to either "the beach" or the name of a specific town. When I was growing up it was common to say "we went to the shore this weekend." When I lived and worked in the Capital, we often said "we went to Bethany this weekend."

The weather cleared some on Saturday morning. I got a great tour from my brother-in-law of the beachfront and the properties now being built. Some of the new homes in the area are astonishing. It appears that the 1990's were very good to those who use the shore as their summer playground. It was also good to some who did not, but do now simply because they have more money than they ever imagined and feel the need to spend it, they buy a house, demolish it and build another the size of a blimp hangar. As I was there shortly after Memorial Day there were many that had been completed only two weeks before. Most were fully landscaped already. We spent some time on our tour calculating the cost of such an endeavor and decided that the sod and trees and annual flowers alone were beyond our means; much less the labor cost of having it put there in a week. One can almost hear the owner explaining to the landscape architect that "Biff and Buffy" and their darling children were coming to help kick off the new place and they simply *must* have the yard finished and not ugly holes and mud and the wretched equipment out there. What will they think? I am sure the laborers were so concerned they only charged two or three times the going rate to get it done. That is why many of the locals now have new fishing boats. As we went through the neighborhoods, there were a few unfinished. At one they had a cement truck pouring the nine yards for the driveway. Can it be imagined what that costs to do on a Saturday morning? These huge homes are on or nearly on the beach and yet the compulsion to landscape them like the any other home does not escape these people. In Delaware, those that were on or near the beach, found the natural sea grass and the sand quite enough. Laying down sod seems silly on many of these properties, but apparently not to the owners. I suppose that when the part of the house that faces the street has the proportions of a courthouse in a small town in Texas, one feels compelled to dress it up.

My brother-in-law decided he must play golf that afternoon and came home soaked through. My sister decided there was no need to go to the club for dinner given the foul weather so we ate at home.

On Sunday, I enjoyed the company of my brother-in-law's brother. We shared sunburn on the back deck while we watched his brother and gracious host, trim bushes and mow the lawn and do other domestic things we felt no compelling reason in which to participate. As noted, I had never been here before and was glad the van was available for living. While I might have managed the house, it was far more comfortable to lie in my own bed and listen to both ocean and rain.

I now understand why they love it in this place so much and why the children return each summer for varying lengths of time to stay with them. The house is less than a block from the beach, but south of the amusements and across the street from a wildlife preserve, complete with a small lake with snapping turtles and fish, where a kayak ride can be enjoyed in the setting sun.

It is very peaceful here. It would have been easy to stay longer and I now know why my brother-in-law finds reasons to come down in the off-season to do projects about the place. The pace is slower then, the climate temperate, and, in another quirk of eastern fashion, "summer" ends on Labor Day. Rarely do seasonal people come after that. The have declared summer over, despite the fact that the water is warmer in

September than in May, as is the weather generally, and the lack of commerce makes it an even more charming place.

I was glad I had finally found my way here after almost 30 years. It is a special place. I could spend my summers in it as my sister does.

Morning would find them on the road back to work and me on my way south to see more children of my sister's progeny as well as returning in a day or two to the Nation's Capital. My hope was that there would be little traffic and the weather would stay cool.

TWENTY

WASHINGTON, D.C.

I traveled the well worn Interstate 95 from New Jersey to reach the outskirts of the Capital City and turned west on I-495, commonly known as "the Beltway." It surrounds the city like a noose around its neck. It makes it possible to go from Baltimore Maryland to Richmond Virginia, and all the way down the Eastern Seaboard for that matter, without having to pass through the city.

Washington is a city that has no direct way through it. If you travel from the north, from Maryland, as I did, you get on the Beltway either headed toward the Maryland suburbs or into Virginia and travel to the nearest likely street that leads you down into the part of town that you want to visit. There are no Interstates that go completely through the Capital, only wide, still handsome (in some cases) Boulevards. When Monsieur L'Enfant, the Frenchman who was commissioned to design the new capital on land donated mostly by Maryland and some from Virginia did it, there was no need for high-speed access. I rather doubt that there was a need for it until well after the Korean War. When I lived here for the 15 years I worked for the legislative branch of the Federal government, it made the commute a challenge. It is a unique city since it is not "in" a state. It is surrounded by two states and exists only because the Continental Congress believed the New Republic needed a " Capital City." I do not think there is another place like it in the world.

Today, the city has one of the best subway systems in the country that seems to go everywhere and there is little need to drive into town unless you work some very strange hours. I was amused when "The Metro" was being built. The people of Washington, who generally are people from other places, were skeptical. The idea of trains running above and below ground to speed them into the city was hard for them to imagine. Having used the New York system so extensively when I was young, it seemed beyond me that it could have critics. There were people who thought it would never work. It was of course built at enormous expense since the city traffic had to be maintained. There are expensive residential areas within the city limits that wanted no part of the construction, or a train station that ran from the ghetto to their corner, for that matter. There were many opponents and much politics involved, but it is hard to imagine how the city would function now without it. For a city laid out as Washington is with a lack of high-speed road access, there is no better way to get to the city to work or play or to visit the remarkable museums. Now that it is done, it is a matter of civic pride, even among many who were skeptical or abhorred the expense.

I followed the Beltway as far as the exit that I used to use to access my neighborhood and got off to see what may have happened to it. I was surprised, particularly given my recent visit to my hometown, to find it so little changed. The first house we had ever owned and lived in for ten years looked about the same. It was still well maintained and most of the landscaping we had done was still there. It seemed I could have gotten out of the van and stepped back to 1980 or so with little trouble. It was still peaceful and some of the same neighbors still lived on the block.

The easiest way to the Virginia suburbs, where my niece, husband and children now lived was to continue through the Maryland section and cross the Potomac River into Virginia on this circular Beltway. The only Interstate, I-66, which actually runs into the city from the north then is available. This road was planned in the 1950's with only one purpose. President Eisenhower instructed his engineers to build a high-speed auto link to the new Dulles International Airport, which at that time seemed to be a long way out in the Virginia countryside. He asked only that one be able to drive to Dulles from downtown in one half-hour. He believed if this could be done the other airport, then known as National and now Reagan National Airport could be closed and the Congressman who wanted to get out of town quickly would have no cause to complain. National Airport is about ten minutes on a good day from the Capitol Building but it also requires an extraordinary approach for pilots down the Potomac River corridor, passing every monument and nearly all the government buildings in the process. It is the second most difficult approach in the country according to the Airline Pilots Association. It is the only one that I am aware of that requires a left hand turn to avoid an Obelisk while on final approach. There are hints that even then the President was uncomfortable about having planes come that close to the White House and the Pentagon building. While there is an absolute prohibition from over flying these and other buildings in the city, it does not take much for an inexperienced pilot to stray a few degrees off course and violate that airspace. But Congressman want to leap in a car and be on a plane in as few minutes as possible. Thus, it survives today.

Because they did complain, and many also lived while in Washington in the fashionable areas through which I-66 would have to be built, along with a host of environmental concerns, the road didn't get finished until the 1980's. By then the route and design were so compromised, it could not fulfill his promise. So it has become a commuter road, like all others. Now, as I drove it, I did note that the Metro runs up the median, but neither it nor the road connect directly to Dulles Airport. Since the area has now been built out, it likely never will.

Design by committee will always run amok. Design with the aid of Congress usually will lead to chaos. The District of Columbia had no self-rule until well into the 1970's. They had no representation in Congress and the residents were only permitted to vote for President. A Congressional Committee that was populated by the same tunnel vision Congressmen from such places as rural Michigan for many years ran it. This is not a recipe for cohesive urban planning.

Since this was Sunday and the roads were familiar, I made good progress and reached my niece's house by early afternoon. She had a driveway of sufficient length and once we figured out how to level the van, it served its purpose well.

I had, oddly, managed to return to a town where I had spent half of my government service without seeing a government building and only a glimpse of the Washington Monument. The city can be peculiar in this way and is more so now since many of the business have relocated to the suburbs for a sheer lack of space in the downtown area. You can be here for a long time and never see those things we associate with the Federal City. My job in the Capitol buildings had made them everyday fixtures for me. Most who work for the "company" in this very company oriented town do see them, but there is a vast group of people who live in the area around Washington to whom the center of the city where the monuments and museums are mean nothing. They go about their lives and only perhaps visit that part of town when friends or relatives come and want to take a tour of "their" Nation's Capital. Or they might go to the fireworks on the Mall every year. The growth of private industry and the support services for the vast suburbs and exurbs of the City now make it possible, I suppose, to spend a whole career in the area without ever having to penetrate the maze of traffic circles and side streets that I had to learn.

I had no desire to take the van downtown where the streets are known for their confusion and, even on the wide Boulevards such as Wisconsin Avenue, some very narrow traffic lanes. I was content to spend my time in the suburbs on the fringe of the city with family and friends rather than tour a museum or the Capital I had been to so many times before.

One of the tricks one learned when visitors came to see the city was to always tell them how great something was that you had not seen before so that you got to see most of the historical places yourself. They could not possibly tour them all in the few days they would be there. This was a way to assure that they got to see the main sights as you drove by and pointed them out, but left you free to go to the Capitol, the National Archives, or one of the many fantastic parts of the vast Smithsonian Institution.

I had dinner one night with some former and present Senate "staffers" that I have known for what seems to be most of my life. We used to kid each other that the workdays were so long there that we actually spent two years working together for every real year that went by. Most that I worked with even during my short return in 1990 and 1991 are not there any longer. The "Hill" is like that. A few stay and love it. They also tutor the young, the ones known as "Kleenex" who come for a few years between law school and a Ph.D. or shortly after, before they try real life. They get the credit on their resume while they work insane hours and then they are gone, used up, after two or three years of 15 hour days and no real personal life.

Of those left, the one in the oddest position that week was one who had worked with me and still was on the staff of the same Committee I worked on last before leaving. He was, on Tuesday, the Minority Counsel to the Ranking Democrat Senator. The Senate was split 51-49

in the Republicans favor at the time. He and his boss were free to criti-
cize and try to amend legislation the Minority did not like and generally
annoy the Majority Party, which is what the Minority Party often does
best. On Wednesday, a Senator from Vermont had an epiphany of sorts
and decided to declare himself an Independent. The Democrats immediately embraced him as a fine fellow and the balance of power shifted
to that party overnight. There was no election; no time lapse between
an election and oath taking that is used in these circumstances to effect
a reasonable transition. By Thursday morning my friend found himself
the Majority Counsel for the now Chairman to whom fell most of the
responsibility for the scheduling of Committee business and legislative
initiatives. It was difficult for me to imagine what a sea change this
would bring to his life. He was having the same problem, but knew as I
did, that he who controls the agenda controls the outcome in many legislative compromises. There also was no guarantee how long this would
last. There were a number of elderly Senators who could go to their just
reward at any time of both political affiliations. Thus, it could all happen again at any time. For a former "staffer", it brings visions of night-
marish gridlock. It is hard to tell, however, whether the rest of the
country that I have been sampling will notice that there has been any
change at all so long as the checks get there on time and we still have a
Department of Defense.

We older staffers (and one or two reasonably young ones) enjoyed
playing "where are they now" and remembering times of outrage and
fun. I made many friends and I hope I helped make a good law or two
while I worked there. But as I listened to the conversation, it was clear
that it was past me now. The only way to keep up is total immersion and
I was sure I had enough of that. I had worked there a long time and,
after my brief return in the early 1990's, I was only sure that I enjoyed
what I was doing instead far more than what I had spent so many years
learning. To be good at "carrying the papers" for a Senator, is a craft that

takes political sense, an ability to know when to be quiet and a certain kind of patience. I have worn out most of those gifts if I ever had them. It is not unusual. The burnout rate is high because the focus and the time commitment are so intense. But I had no reason to feel that I would want to do it again and marveled some at those who have done it for so long.

I do not wish to suggest that doing it was not fun. There is that too. Nevertheless, it is very easy to become insulated in Washington and to believe that what you are working on is important to every single person in the country and they know all about it. After all, it is one of the few professions that one can work in where what is happening in the place you work is reported on the front page of most newspapers everyday. This can lead to a belief that it is very important and that the answers only lay here in the Halls of Congress, the White House and the Executive Agencies and with the Supreme Court. When you leave you find out it isn't true, but the will to leave is not strong when you are dealing day to day with the heady stuff of national policy. Those politicians who understand that the power to make law may be here, but the implementation of it is local are the ones that do best. The staff people are the same. They can become so full of their own importance that they cannot see that what they say or do matters little to my friends Buddy and Dot and many others.

There are many funny moments in a career here, some which are that way simply because they are unexpected. We as a Nation, tend to lavish an amount of respect upon our elected officials that they do not deserve as individuals but that is part of the mantel of the office. I have seen people diametrically opposed to the views of a Senator treat him or her with the utmost courtesy when given the chance to shake hands. We can often forget they are people like us with a particular talent that we may not have, but may lack those that we do. They are quite human, capable of humor and pathos and genuine caring for others that some find strange when it rises to public attention. Perhaps when they are home in their districts or states, the people they know well see it. When they are on the political stage that is Washington, glimpses of it come rarely and we are surprised.

Each of us that spent time "staffing" a Senator has a collection of anecdotal glimpses of such humor. The Canadians by the way, have a term for such staff people as I was who do the heavy lifting and serve as a public official's subject expert and liaison with lobbyists and others. The call them "Sherpas", as those who carry the burden up the Himalayans are known. It seems quite apt and I am not surprised that they, who may be more facile with language than we are, came up with it.

Some of us who met that night had been in government service when the Watergate scandal took place. I was already working on Capital Hill at the time. It is likely the largest political story reported in the last century. There is not now, nor was there then, a lack of gallows humor in Washington. It is famous for that art form. Some of it was quite spontaneous. There were so many shocking things that surrounded Watergate and all that word meant that it became hard to take it all in as it ground on to its' inevitable conclusion. After the initial shock, a grim reality set in that this was indeed a Constitutional crisis and that these men that I worked among every day would have to solve it. One way to deal with that burden was to deflect it with humor.

In a time before the public was "invited" through the passage of the so-called "sunshine laws" to watch the final drafting of a bill, Committee Members met in closed rooms with only staff present. Things were said there that are not said today with lobbyists and the press in the room. I assure you, very few members of the public ever come and the "sunshine" may be the single leading cause of the demise of the quick compromise. In the fall of 1972, Mr. Nixon's Vice President, Spiro T. Agnew resigned in the face of allegations of irregularities in his campaigns and businesses. Perhaps many saw this coming, but I admit that I did not. While sitting in a full closed Committee meeting trying to finalize the Senate version of a bill that would decide the role of the federal government in primary and secondary education, which was a matter of some gravity, Senators and staff were gathered around a very large square of tables that had been pushed together. The Senators sat on the side that their party affiliation dictated and in descending order of committee seniority. The staff was busy briefing their bosses on possible amendments and whispering to other staff, shoring up support for their own changes among their bosses while the Senator's were signing mail or reading a newspaper. That is not to suggest that they were not engaged, since I have seen them come from what appeared to be total distraction to full attention in a nanosecond when it mattered, but at the moment only preliminary courtesies and skirmishes were going on before the real thing got started.

I noticed that a subcommittee counsel who was not engaged in this particular piece of business had entered the room and was whispering in the Chairman's ear. After a moment, the Chairman suggested that the counsel had an announcement to make. This particular Democratic Counsel was legendary for his twisted sense of humor and sarcastic manner, so it was not a surprise that he made two. He said, to the best of my recollection: "Senators, the Vice President has resigned, and the Mets are losing 2-1." After what seemed like a stunned silence of many seconds, one of the Senators, who had been studying the New York Times Crossword puzzle and smoking a crooked Italian cigar, looked up and said: "What inning is it?" The remark filled the room with bipartisan laughter from us all. More importantly, it broke the tension for all of them at a time when that was what they needed more than partisanship or pompous speeches. Soon the doors would open and each would face the press to "react to this stunning development" as the press would put it and they needed a moment like this to get them through it. I believe it is often how they survive the seething caldron of public exposure and scrutiny and is only an example of how it was sometimes done. All staffers have favorite moments like that when it seemed that humor was what was needed most.

That night we shared some of those moments. I enjoyed hearing them because it brought back the good times. It was what made us stick together through the long days and nights of writing Committee reports and redrafting legislation under impossible deadlines. The laughs were not as frequent as we liked, but they made the place seem saner.

I repaired to the quiet driveway in the suburbs where, for this town built largely on a swamp, the weather was remarkably pleasant. I stayed there for the rest of my visit enjoying the children and my niece's and her husband's good cooking. It had been fun to revisit and enjoy some memories and revile others, but it had been enough.

The oldest child, a daughter, has grown from an infant to nearly three since last we met. She is quite the lady. The youngest, a boy is new to me and, at one, to the rest of the world as well. He is agreeable and well mannered. I threatened to take him home with me. I am sure that this stage in his life will pass and he will move on like all other children. He is precious at the moment .As always, my family saw to it that I was well cared for and sent home early to my dwelling.

There was an Oriole game on Sunday but I passed in favor of going a few minutes up the road to spend the night and part of a day with my good friend and mentor from my days in the Capital and his wife. He was my friend and Chief Counsel and left the Hill when he was appointed a Federal Judge. We had dinner and caught up on many things and the next morning we explored the world of politics and what had happened in our personal lives. Then I was off late Monday morning to continue north and west while he went back to writing an opinion for the court. It was a pleasant time. The weather continues to cooperate and I am headed through Maryland and Pennsylvania again. This time, it will be in the western part of the Pennsylvania searching out some childhood summer memories and then north and west. It is still dry, but the heat increases as the inevitable summer comes.

TWENTY-ONE

BEDFORD, BUTLER, AND THE LINCOLN HIGHWAY

There are two facts that one cannot escape in this part of Pennsylvania. It is old and poor. Coal and steel made it what it was. Steel is gone and coal is still as hazardous a way to make a living as it always was. It is also less preferred as a type of fuel these days, so while the hills may remain rich with it, less is taken out. The infrastructure is circa 1950-60 and getting no better. The roads will rattle your teeth and there is little, other than the haunting rural beauty of its lakes and farms, to recommend a trip through here at all. I am certain there are well meaning people who care deeply about individuals with disabilities, but thus far whatever efforts they have made to ensure compliance with laws of accessibility here have made only a small dent. Compliance by municipalities and the Turnpike Authority with the Americans with Disabilities Act is appalling and the reactions to any comments to the contrary are met with indifference or defensiveness. It is sad. It is also illegal. It would be nice if all those compassionate people would talk to their elected officials, maybe drop a Senator a line about enforcing the laws they pass. They are, after all the alleged defenders of the halt and the lame and were there and voted for the Act when it passed Congress, in most cases. The state gets my vote for the northern state with the least. My view is quite biased, I realize, but it is mine and there it is.

Pittsburgh and Philadelphia may be the bookends and modern and quite charming in their way, but there is precious little in between except those hauntingly lovely hills, small farms and Amish villages.

Once again I search out memories. Traveling the U.S. routes and doing everything possible to avoid the Pennsylvania Turnpike, I leave a friendly Maryland near Hagerstown, where, while stopping for lunch, six people welcomed me to the state or asked for tours of the "rig you have there." In a further bizarre moment, two men who comment on it turn out to be employed as drivers of new motor coaches for a company ten minutes from the factory where mine is made. They are both from Fargo, North Dakota and sound like it. Thanks to one of my former secretaries who grew up in Two Rivers Wisconsin, I recognized the accent immediately. They implored me to come visit the prairie on my way home. Cool air and few people are the attractions. One has to appreciate many miles of slightly rolling hills covered with amber waves of grain to make that trip. I am thinking about it.

Largely unknown by even members of my generation, I suspect, is that the Pennsylvania Turnpike, which I am so quick to vilify, was the first high speed, limited access toll road in the country. It was built along an existing railroad bed, which had been abandoned by one of the robber Baron railroad entrepreneurs. When it opened, it had tunnels of one lane in each direction, hairpin turns and steep grades, which still exist except for the tunnels, that have either been bypassed, or a new one was drilled next to the old to increase the flow in each direction. It is mostly two lanes in the western part and the roadbed is eaten once a year by salt, plows, and too many trucks. It is almost beyond comprehension that when it opened, it had no speed limit at a time long after Model T's had left service. It is an abdominal road, which again is saved only by the scenery one passes when you travel it.

I digress. I came through this way because it was convenient and to look at some places of my distant past. My father had a business associate who had a cottage near a town called Derry. It is near Latrobe, the birthplace of Arnold Palmer and Rolling Rock Beer (not necessarily in chronological order). It is also on U.S. 30, the Old Lincoln Highway. It is to folks in this neighborhood what U.S. 66 is to the nostalgia buffs in California. It was the first of the "national roads" built sometime early in the last century to move the new motorcar and truck across this then steel and coal producing behemoth of a state and beyond to the east coast. It continues on from here across the country and I would see parts of it still well preserved as far away as Nebraska. There is a section north of Bedford that runs through the hills and farming towns that is a delight. By noon, however, it had become a strip mall paradise on the outskirts of one of the larger towns on the way to Pittsburgh. Between the two is Derry. It is a lovely little town that has changed little. The bridge over the railroad tracks that I remember as made of wood, which had spaces between its' great slabs, that scared the cheese out of a certain seven year-old, is now concrete. There are lovely playing fields of all types that grace the edge of the town, but the church (standard issue red brick, large steeple of steel) remains, as do many of the houses. Unfortunately, I did not find the site of the cabin in the deep woods that we used for two weeks every July. It is now gone, I believe, and the place where the entrance used to leave the highway is Idyllwild, a very large amusement park. It could well be the largest and only one in the western part of the state judging by the crowds showing up on a weekday. This was the site of the "camp" as they are called here, with cottages on the hill with great screened in sleeping porches and few amenities. It was a great place to let your kids run in those days, with a pool and lots of woods. It was owned by a Christian church, which had an amphitheater in the middle of the place. People came and went to services there all day and half the night on Sunday. We only knew of those of course, since we were Catholics and not permitted to mingle. My most vivid memories of the place were my Mother telling me of the Armistice that ended the Korean War in the kitchen, and once every summer, my father would take me to Pittsburgh with him and the trip would include a Pirate baseball game at old Forbes Field. The Pennsylvania Railroad also passed nearby and in the evening we would go watch the trains. My first imaginary journeys took place on those trains as I watched them pass in the twilight there. The cottages had screened eating areas and when there was a birthday, each family in turn would sing to the lucky devil that had been born in July. This was a mountain paradise. Many like it still exist and, as I said, are the only reason I can think of to come here.

U.S. 22, a northern route, leads eventually to Erie, PA. It is a piece of real estate that Pennsylvania insisted on keeping back when it needed a port to access the Great Lakes. I traveled some of the road to see if it was still as neglected as the last time I was on it thirty years ago, and to reach a campground in Butler. The road was worse than I remembered and the campground was not like any I have been in on the trip.

The Buttercup Resort Camp is on RV Lane on the outskirts of Butler. It is really two parks, one, which is "gated" and appears to have permanent "trailers" parked in it. It is wooded and shaded and everyone seems to own a golf cart to get to the pool and other places. The other part is a vast grassy knoll that has many hook ups and few visitors which is pretty much out in the open. I had to call the owner on my cell phone since the thirty steps leading to the office pretty much kept me out of there, despite the notation in the trailer guide as "handicap access." He graciously appeared five minutes later to ask if I had a reservation. I explained that it is not my personal habit to show up unannounced unless the campground specifically states in the *Trailer Life* Directory that it does not accept reservations. After determining that I may or may not (in his view) have called the previous Saturday and been told I would not likely need a reservation, he allowed as how he had a space and that he took only cash.

Well. I had been out in the 85 degree heat too long for much more of this nonsense, so I asked why, since, his little piece of paradise was listed as having "handicap access", there was no ramp? I also inquired as to

141 / *Michael W. Burns*

what time he expected the 100 or so others that night to fill his last spaces here in paradise or did he do reservation only business? For some reason he got both accommodating and defensive after that and told me about his lovely restrooms. They had full access, but they were also inside the gate, by the way, and I was not likely to get anywhere near them. He then took me halfway up the hill, picked a spot seemingly at random (in the shade, but halfway down the hill from the restrooms on this side) took my $18.00 for a full hookup, mumbled something about coming to get him if I needed him (guess he forgot the steps) and left.

There were two more campers that checked in after me so the grassy acres looked a little like the plains of Africa as the sun set and the air cooled enough to allow a number of the golf carts owners to drive up the hill and inspect the new arrivals. I cancelled the idea of spending another night and decided to keep moving. I left early, before most, if not all, of the permanent villagers were up and about.

Goodbye, Pennsylvania. It wasn't great, but it could have been worse. The lyrical names of the towns in the western part left there by the Amish—Mars, Apollo and more remain. The greatness has faded. Perhaps someday there will be a new industrial revolution and this area will be a part of it. Once, that is, the current denizens get over the fact that the factory that closed in 1980 isn't coming back anytime soon. There were many other parts of the trip that I enjoyed more than this one, and some were even in Pennsylvania. Unfortunately, this last view of the state did not leave me with a good feeling about the place.

TWENTY-TWO

MILAN, OHIO

Leaving Pennsylvania the weather turned oppressively hot. I also felt the beginnings of a head cold. The campground I was to visit next was on Lake Erie, It was a state campground with no services listed and I did not think I would survive without conditioned air part of the time. It also was a "no reservation" site and I judged that by the time I was at the turn, it was likely I was going to make the 25 mile drive to the Lake only to find that it was full given that the weekend was coming and the heat was here. I had been interested in going there only because the last time I had been through here there were rivers that flowed into the lake that caught fire from all the pollution. I know great strides had been made and the lake and its' islands were once again pleasurable places to visit in summer.

Now, however, it seemed perfectly rational to get off the Interstate and take refuge in an air-conditioned motel and catch up with mail and personal hygiene before moving on to Michigan. When it hit 96 at midday I thought I had made the right decision. If I had not been rushing to reach the campground early, I might have found alternate routes to avoid joining Interstate 80 at the Pennsylvania state line, but the sudden head cold lessened my interest in circuitous routes, so listening to CDs while on cruise control was easier while taking sinus medication.

The Ohio Turnpike has always been designated Interstate 80. It was continued through northern Pennsylvania some years ago to give the traveler a more direct route into the New York Metropolitan area. It replaced the maligned (at least by me) Pennsylvania Turnpike as the route of choice for many trucks, buses and vacationers. Because of the peculiarity in its construction along the old railroad right of way, there was no option to widen the Turnpike.

The Ohio Turnpike seems to suffer the affliction of constant repairs. It seems to have been undergoing cosmetic surgery for as long as I can remember. You get the feeling that the state wants to make a good impression. Except for the usual wear and tear caused by all that tonnage moving at high speed, the road always seems in good shape. Yet they repair lanes, add lanes, and cause reduced speeds constantly. They must have a Member of Congress on the right committee since they never cease to have money for this endeavor. I had not been on it for years since my days of traveling from Maryland to Chicago, but my brother, who used it extensively to return to see family in New Jersey from Michigan, will testify that it has been this way for as long as he can remember. It is not a big deal in the larger worldview, but an interesting—and annoying circumstance. Miles of "Right Lane Closed" signs are not a favorite sight for most drivers when it requires them to lower speeds and they are strictly enforced. It is also difficult at times to find more than one work crew in a ten-mile stretch of this annoyance doing anything more than driving a pickup truck in the closed lane with the lights flashing.

I had about enough for the day in Huron County at the Huron River not yet in Sandusky. When I exited, I saw a sign for the "Birthplace of the Man of the Millennium, Thomas A. Edison." There were several things that intrigued me about this. I had no idea, having grown up near Edison New Jersey, that Edison had been born here. Further, I didn't remember that anyone named him the Man of the Millennium. Perhaps the town where he was born had a special election. It seemed presumptuous to simply declare Thomas Alva Edison the Man of the Millennium, as great as he and his inventions might have been.

So it was a chance heat wave, a full camp ground, and a decision that I wanted to stop and tend to my head cold rather than continue on to the home of the Toledo Mud Hens baseball team that led me, later in the day, to a place that looked for all the world like a town I would see in Connecticut.

Milan Ohio is charming with a rich and varied history, which, by accident of his father's occupations and the political allegiances of his forefathers, was the place where one of the greatest inventors of all time was born.

Milan justifiably bills itself as a picturesque town, both the birthplace of Edison and a remarkable place of growth and history as an inland canal port. It was settled by white missionaries, the Monrovians, who lived among the Indians in a village known as Petquotting, in 1787. This is now the site of Milan. They left, for unexplained reasons, in 1804. Milan is in what is known as the Firelands, the western most tract of a parcel of land known as the Connecticut Western Reserve. The name is apt since it was land given to Connecticut families burned out of their homes and driven west during the Revolutionary War.

The Huron River was navigable to Lake Erie in the early 1800's to within three miles of Milan. Daring entrepreneurs decided that they would build a canal from the town to the river and thus access the Lake. By 1839 the first ship from the Great Lakes entered the canal, and this once quiet inland village where one of the first settlers, Ebenezer Merry, had built a flower and saw mill in 1816 now became a hub of commerce for the western United States. Warehouses were built nearly overnight to store the 300,000 bushels of grain. Hundreds of wagons from 150 miles away lined the roads daily to unload the grain from the inland farms to be shipped through Milan to the cities of the north and east. More ships were needed to move the grain than entered the canal, so Milan began building them. By 1847 more than 75 schooners had been built and were under sail. In 1847, more than 917,800 bushels of wheat were shipped from this port, making it the second largest in the world after the Ukrainian city of Odessa.

Milan was content and on its' way to becoming a port city of huge importance in the northeast. But then came the railroad. Milan fought the introduction of rail transportation for obvious economic reasons. But rails, not canals, were the future, and it lost. By 1869, Milan's canal and warehouses were being abandoned to become part of the village's history. One warehouse still stands near the canal basin in mournful testimony to the times of plenty.

Even without the presence of the Edison family, this would still be a remarkable village. This meteoric burst of commerce made many rich, and left as quickly as it came, and yet a lovely town, with homes representative of those boom times remains. It is part of Ohio history and a proud chapter in the history of Huron County. Yet millions pass within 7 miles of its bucolic town square every year and have no idea it is there, what it was, or what it has become. I thought of it in the same way that I thought of being in a plane, flying at 500 miles an hour over a land so rich and diverse and interesting. Those who travel the "I" roads travel in the same sort of hermetically sealed existence. They go fast, eat plastic food, and never know of Ebenezer Merry, or see the place where Edison was born. We learn to travel quickly and efficiently, but as a result there is so much we know nothing about.

The town square is the centerpiece, where there is a bandstand any New England town would be proud to have; a monument to both those who died and survived the Civil War from Milan; and a statue of a young Mr. Edison reading at his mother's knee. There is the Town Hall that was built in 1864 and has the same façade as it had then. There are shops and buildings that are not "faux" replicas, but lovingly cared for originals. There are period lampposts that are of course now electric, which border the square, each donated in memory of some citizens who were perhaps prominent and perhaps not. On another side, the Milan Inn stands looking as if it would open for dinner, with vases and linen on the tables in the first floor dining room. The second floor looks ready for guests as well. All the rooms that faced the square had welcoming candles in the windows in the Amish tradition. I was assured by one of the nice ladies who worked in City Hall that it still was used for "occasions", although it did not open regularly. It badly needed a coat of paint, but otherwise looked like I imagined it did in the 1800's.

Down the street is the old canal basin and near it the place where Edison was born. He did not live here long, his great- grandfather John Edison was an inventor too, and had lived in New Jersey during colonial times. Some 160 years later, the tract of land that John had farmed back there was where Thomas made his home. John Edison was a loyalist during the Revolution, and like most who stayed true to King George, soon took refuge in Nova Scotia, after having his property confiscated under tenuous legal circumstances and sentenced to be executed. His prominent relatives saw to it that he made it safely to Canada but the family fortunes fluctuated after that. Edison's grandfather, a Canadian by birth, served in the British Navy in the War of 1812. His father married the daughter of one of Washington's officers. He left Canada after an unsuccessful attempt to free the country from British Rule and finally settled in Milan where he made roof shingles and Thomas eventually joined his mother and five siblings when born on February

11,1847. Seven years later they were back on the New Jersey land and the house passed on to other owners until one of his sisters bought it and lived there for a time. Edison became the owner himself in 1906. He never lived there. On a visit in 1926 he was a bit shocked to find that one of his properties, of all places, was one of the few left in Milan still lit by gas lamps and candles.

This place is full of history. It was for a few years one of the great ports of the world. It was the birthplace of the man who invented the telephone, the phonograph, a way to record votes electronically, wireless telegraphy, the electric pen used in mimeograph machines, the motion picture camera, the miner's lamp, the nickel iron-alkaline storage battery and vulcanized rubber among other things. The town sits quietly near a roaring Interstate, quaint for its history, but lovely in its present state and unknown to most outside of Huron County.

The centerpiece of the town is without doubt the village green. It has that imposing monument to those who fought in the Civil War. At its base are the names of all the battles they fought in as part of various Ohio Regiments and an obelisk that rises above to which is affixed the "Roll Call of the Dead." Unusual for such structures is that there is also a "Roll Call of the Living." The fellow who was cutting the lawn when I arrived, explained that this honored the men who returned to Milan and in many cases became its' leading citizens and businessmen, who took their place in the town as they would have had there not been a war. There were small plaques in the grass at the base that honored those who had served in World War One and Two. I asked him why there were none for Korea or Vietnam. He looked into the distance and said there had been some talk about that but the American Legion, which provided the other two, and whose local Post was in one of the buildings facing the square, had donated the ones that were there. He did not elaborate. I hoped that the Charles Evans American Legion

Post is chronically short of cash, or just takes its' time to deliberate about such things. I hoped that, but doubted it provided a plausible explanation.

Leaving now, on a stifling hot day in northern Ohio, a soft breeze blowing in the shade on the village green, having had a wonderful time discovering all this and talking to some of the friendly people, I marveled at how much I had enjoyed this day simply because it was on the way, and I took the time to get off the highway and find it.

TWENTY-THREE

MICHIGAN AND ILLINOIS

Some of the stops along the way do not seem fair. Mainly, because they are too short. Leaving Ohio for Grand Blanc Michigan was a race to beat the weather. The oppressive heat continued. Relief was coming in the form of a fairly violent front, so the only question was whether I made the destination, waited for it to go through or caught the weather on the road. Although still entirely too hot, getting there ahead of it seemed the best idea.

After a short stretch of Ohio Turnpike to Toledo and the home of my beloved Mud Hens, along with thousands of other Friday travelers I headed north in Michigan, traveling up U.S.23 through Ann Arbor and beyond. I was not going all that far beyond but the folks on the road with me, with boats and trailers in tow, were on their way to Traverse City and the "Upper Peninsula" where they spend many of their weekends. The part of the state above Mackinaw really has never had any business being part of Michigan. It has threatened to secede every now and then, has tried to join Wisconsin in the past and rejected Daylight Savings Time claiming the cows could not cope with 10 PM sunsets. It is cool in summer and many natives have second homes there. No one, except those who live or must do business there, goes in winter except the snowmobile people who enjoy racing on vast expanses of flatlands.

The weather front came through soon after I arrived that evening and I enjoyed wonderful weather the rest of the visit. I was here to see my brother, his wife and their youngest son. All but son would be headed to Denver the following week to see number one son who was the one kind enough to construct the website where I posted information about the stops on my journey. Gracious hosts always, they only lacked a level driveway. We enjoyed dinners and number two son explained materials engineering and golf to me. He knows a great deal about both and actually makes me understand some of it. He also understands a lot about music and has a band. He recently recorded a CD that he gave me so I could hear his work out on the open road. With all these vocations and avocations he is hardly the typical engineer. It was a pleasant if short visit. The Tigers were on the road, so I miss yet another new stadium.

Tuesday found me in Chicago and a visit with my wife's side of the family. Here, as in Grand Blanc, the time was short but the company gracious and the weather held reasonably cool and clear. My brother-in-law is a pilot and I usually get in at least one flying session in with him to remind me how to do it. However, my head cold kept me grounded and, alas, the Cubs left town the day before, so another ballpark, one of the originals, is missed. Lots of bad timing.

It was back out on the road by Thursday as the trip of now some 6,500 miles continues. The visits with family have been a wonderful renewal of friendships. Now I am back on the road in the same way that I was in the early stages of the trip. I must find my conversations with strangers and move across the vast Midwest looking for things that may be of interest. I have returned to the other part of the journey. I will not see family again for about ten days when I reach Colorado. I have had the chance to renew friendships and family ties. In some cases I have met children who I had never met before. There have been places I had not been in a long time, or have never seen. There have been people like the Mayor, Dot, and Buddy and many, many more. I will add to these now as I move on. Inevitably, this must all come to an end. But for now, it is not over. There will be many people to meet and places yet to see that will be a wonder to my eyes. As I go on to Iowa, South Dakota, Wyoming and Colorado, I have yet to grow tired of living in my small fiberglass house. I still enjoy it and do not want to miss what I know will still be interesting places and people.

TWENTY-FOUR

THE BIRTHPLACE OF "DUTCH"; A FIELD OF DREAMS; AND LOOKING FOR RADAR O'REILLY

I left Chicago in a downpour. Heading west, a short detour to Dixon leads to Ronald Reagan's birthplace. Having been to the "place called Hope" earlier, it seemed only fair to give equal time to the birthplace of Mr. Reagan. It is amazing. I would not even ask where the money came from, but surely not from the taxpayers of Dixon. It is a lovely setting, even in the rain. The admission is free, the people are kind, and the artifacts interesting.

Mr. Reagan's early years during the Depression and his many hardships and jobs, and the lack of them, are well chronicled. His early radio days, when he re-created baseball and football games on WOC in Davenport by reading with feeling, what the wire service account described. Many announcers around the country did these "recreations." They narrated what had just happened. They then whacked a stick on the desk (if it was baseball) and making a noise that loosely resembles a crowd roar to signal that it was a hit. He made this thing that happened perhaps five minutes before sound very exciting. Their worst nightmare of these early announcers was a ticker carrying the running commentary from the site that stopped for some reason.

"Vamping" about foul balls, a mythical three-ball count on the batter and other ways to kill time occurred while they silently prayed for the thing to start again. Mr. Reagan used to recount stories about how it happened to him and how many "foul balls" a batter might have to hit before the ticker brought the real news to him again. Eventually, WOC became WHO which is one of the most powerful radio stations in the Mid-West. He was apparently there for the transition.

My detour to Dyersville just west of Dubuque Iowa, reached by the "river route" along the Mississippi was in much the same weather. The river and its barge traffic rolls on and is quite beautiful if only in just knowing, having earlier been to Vicksburg, how far it travels and the amount of commerce that it carries now and how much more it did before railroads, trucks, and airplanes.

I now have at least seen the ballpark that I hoped I would. There, on the 90-year-old Lansing Farm is the baseball diamond "created" by the Kevin Costner character in the movie "Field of Dreams." It has become a Mecca of the purists of baseball. I will only try summarizing the movie plot for those of you who may not have seen it. Suffice to say that among baseball fans it is a cult film. It either originated or made famous the phrase, "if you build it, they will come". A farmer built the field in the middle of his farm and all the greats of the game came and played, including his father. They came and went through the cornstalks that line the outfield.

My short time there was ghostly. The mist that shrouded the field made it seem quite possible to me that at any moment "Shoeless "Joe Jackson or another of the greats of long ago would walk out of the corn stalks and take his place in the batter's box. It is a remarkable place, made perhaps less so by the folks who "saved" it. The attendant commercialism is not very pleasing, and there are suits and counter- suits that abound as what belongs to whom and who has the rights to what. All rather tawdry and only reinforces a core belief that greed drives the world. I was largely able to avoid all this unpleasantness and the attendant commercialism. It was a quiet weekday morning in the rain and a few pilgrims stood there with me. I came away with no overpriced T-Shirt or hat to proclaim my attendance, only a memory of a verdant field and the possibility of a game to be played by the greats from the past. It does give you the surreal feeling that it could happen here.

It was a short trip to Davenport towards my original destination of Des Moines. A glance at the map told me I was not far from Ottumwa, Iowa, home of the mythical Radar O'Rielly from the television series M*A*S*H. Radar was played by Gary Burghoff who was the nephew of a man I worked with for a number of years. Gary now lives in Connecticut. The character's special naiveté made him hard not to like. He was, in the long running series, the company clerk that kept the unit alive and in bandages and whatever else it needed. He was the Patron saint of Staff People. Since this had been my vocation most of the last 28 years. I could relate to Radar. He was the ultimate "staffer."

The story line was that his Mother and Uncle Ed ran the family farm in Ottumwa where other strange members of his family also lived. Eventually, Uncle Ed dies, and Radar goes home to run the farm. He is, it turns out, less successful in this than in keeping a Mobile Hospital running. I went there to ask where the O'Rielly farm might be. I got some smiles, some frowns, and ignored a lot. One man named Richard at the place where I took on fuel finally reacted as I had hoped and gave me precise directions to the farm, although he said that Radar did not live there anymore, having retired to Florida a few years ago. It was impressive. He never cracked, but remained as serious as one could be about a real person. Following his directions, I found a farm, which I dutifully photographed. Too bad Radar wasn't there. There was a lot I wanted to ask him. It was clear that I was not the first who had wandered through with these questions about a fictional character. I am not sure that some who have asked before me did not actually believe there was a Radar and a farm and the rest, which may have accounted for the looks I got from some I asked.

The story got more interesting when, as I traveled through Denver later in the trip, I told this story to my niece, who related that Mr. Burghoff now lives quite near her Mother in Connecticut and I met a physician who was a member of her practice, who had grown up in Ottumwa and had apparently put up with a good bit of this all her life.

Ottumwa is hardly a small town. It is a small city. It may have been much smaller in the time of Korea, or the M*A*S*H creators may have just assumed it. It is known as the "City of Bridges" according to the visitor center on the way to town. There are three that span the Des Moines River. The town was born a river port in 1851. Ottumwa means "rippling waters" in one language or another and one of the bridges, the Jefferson Viaduct, is said to be the longest municipally owned bridge in the state. I did not measure it so will take the Chamber of Commerce's word for it. The carnival was also in a park near the river, and on an early summer's day, it was an inviting place to stop, eat, and watch people for a while.

I went back north to a less crowded place to my destination for the night near Des Moines. The weather was clear and cool when I made the campsite in Kellogg. It was near Interstate 80, but on the edge of a farm. It had a place to park, electricity and some lovely old trees. Its lack of "amenities" was pleasing for a change.

I sat out and watched the sunset as cars went by on the not too nearby road, dreaming up destinations for them and watching a glorious sunset. It was then to bed in my own field of dreams. The cornfield came up to the edge of the camp's access road. It was a lovely, simple setting to sleep, perchance to dream of baseball games of long ago.

-2-

The last two of my adventures in Iowa, which may seem an oxymoron to some given its reputation as a flat and vast wasteland, took me through John Wayne's (aka Marion Morrison's) birthplace. The other was in search of the Bridges of Madison County. This was done at what seemed like warp speed since I now remember little of the first, although it was hardly the largest tourist attraction in the state. It was interesting only in the sense that it was another example of someone who, despite humble beginning, became an American icon for more than half a century.

Madison County is another story. The covered bridges there were made famous, or perhaps infamous, by the novel and subsequent movie, "The Bridges of Madison County." Both had less to do with the bridges than the brief relationship of a man who had come there to photograph them and a woman who had been on the farm way too long. I confess that I never saw the movie. I read the book because it took two hours to do so and I was looking for something to read and wondered what all the fuss was about. After reading it, I am still not sure.

There are, apparently, what Iowans think are a large number of covered bridges in Madison County. I don't think folks in Vermont would agree with that, but the Amana Colonies appear to all have them and there were others. I went to Winterset—where the movie was filmed in part—which proclaimed it was the "Gateway to the Bridges of Madison County." Aside from the fractured language, it was true that, having been in Madison County for about an hour, I did see my first covered bridge. I also saw a building that was described as the visitor's center for the bridges. I had now spent as much time looking around as I had spent reading the book and decided I had, in my life, seen about as many covered bridges as I needed and decided to leave for lunch. It was, I will admit, a lovely place in Iowa, but I was hungry and whatever romance the bridges represented had left me. Since the book was fiction, only the bridges can be touted as attractions. I found one that looked legitimate, took a picture of it and left.

TWENTY-FIVE

YANKTON, SOUTH DAKOTA

About the time I was eating lunch in western Iowa, I realized it was 2 PM on Friday and except for moving to the western side of the state I had made no progress at all towards my next stop in South Dakota. The vastness of space in the Upper Midwest was suddenly upon me and I was very late in getting started. As near as I could tell, my destination just beyond Yankton in the Lewis and Clarke Recreation Areas was still more than 200 miles away. By the time I got to the Omaha area I realized that might be conservative, so grinding away at high speed and seeing little from there on I went north through Sioux City (not to be confused with Sioux Falls) and on to Yankton and a bit beyond. Generally, this is not the sort of drive I would make on Friday, but campsites were scarce and I had read that this was as nice a recreation area as there was in the eastern part of South Dakota. Neither the campsite nor the people disappointed me.

I am not sure I had yet seen a campsite as vast. There are actually six areas along the river. The state took over three this spring. One is still run by the Army Corps of Engineers. One, on the other side of the river is actually in Nebraska and also run by the Corps. There are a number of these around the country. The Corps built them usually as part of a dam project, this time on the Missouri River. They are all well built, and maintained. The states are now taking most of them over since the federal government is getting out of the campsite business, so how long they stay as nice as they are will depend on local funding and interest. The morning after I got in I was talking to one of the "rangers" who told me that they had turned ten RVs away the night before. This vast campground was full, with the exception of a few tenting only sites that were reserved for today's arrivals. Many local people, when summer begins to fill these places on weekends, will pay for an extra day to hold it for their arrival. Some locals will drive two hours or more on a Wednesday or Thursday night, pay the fee, drop their trailer in the site they like, and go back home. They return Friday or Saturday and don't have to worry about being in a site they don't like. I am sure many have used the same one for years.

This was a mixed-use area called Pierson Ranch. It is next to the lake, pleasantly shaded and offers electricity, public baths and restrooms and whatever you bring with you. I soon learned one thing they all brought here was about a cord of wood. Everyone seems to cook outdoors, most on wood fires that fill the air and thus the van with an acrid smell. Others use grills shaped like beer kegs, painted with the brewery label that seems, to them at least, clever. One is far enough south here that the "Fargo" accent is less apparent. Most root for the "Twins" and the "Vikings", but the age old rivalry between the states remains. Minnesotans don't think the folks who live in "the Dakotas" are very bright, and these folks respond with more than an occasional crack about how you can't find something or other over in Minnesota. The town of Vermillion is right down the road and that is where the University is. I am sure the locals don't think of it as being isolated, but it is a long drive from Sioux City. It is almost funny to an urbanite like me to see a Dome for the athletic field "out in the middle of nowhere." There is a seminary in Yankton for Benedictines and Mount Marty College. It is named after a very famous Cardinal who was here for a very long time. None of the campers seemed to know much more than that.

The Sioux Nation made its last stand in this state. It is the place of Little Big Horn and Wounded Knee, two ends of the spectrum for the Nation, the zenith and the nadir for Sitting Bull and his brave warriors and their people.

When summer comes here, particularly after a winter like the last, the natives seize it with zeal even greater than in New England. They seem to remain in perpetual motion and out doors for as long as possible. They have toys to go camping, they fish and boat and spend hours on bicycles, circling the campgrounds and the recreation areas. I watched a volleyball game in the day area that must have set a record for time on a 90-degree day that was as competitive as anything a Californian has seen on one of their beaches.

The "curiosity" factor about me seems to diminish in direct proportion to my proximity to the West Coast. After all, these folks have seen California plates more often than the people in Rotterdam, New York. However, a man in a wheelchair traveling alone will always bring curiosity. The kind people of South Dakota are less direct in their approach, perhaps reflecting their own self-reliant and gentle nature in this land of extreme weather and vast distances between towns and each other. Those I spoke to were friendly and interesting. Not surprisingly, a child was the first to approach. He announced that he was Mitchell and he was bored. I guess that made me interesting. He told me about the trailer his family has which is only "three days old" and how he and his brother got to sleep in it the night they brought it home. A bit later, his mother came looking for him. She tells of having camped in tents and "pop up" trailers for years and deciding to buy a large new trailer only last week. This is its' first trip. She finds my months on the road interesting. I find the fact that she was born and raised in a town of less than 100 people more fascinating to me. She invites me to join the rest of the family for "smores", a concoction of Hershey bars and graham crackers that I decline, partly because of the chocolate content, but mostly due to my weariness for having clocked so many miles that day.

Late morning the next day finds me in Yankton at the grocery store. It is a chain common here called HYVEE. Except for avocados, it has everything anyone could want to eat. This is a very historic and interesting town, but understated. I wandered through a good bit of it before I went back to camp. There are casinos everywhere, very small ones, some even attached to gas stations. Of course these are Sioux lands so I assumed I will see them. But I did not see a big one like we have near home, just the small, almost unobtrusive ones in town. The River District is interesting. Because it is on the Missouri River, Yankton was at one time a very important place for the shipment of upper Midwest grain and other food grown by the eastern European and Scandinavian farmers that had settle here one the edge of the Indian territories. The Dakotas came to the United States as part of the Louisiana Purchase and petitioned early to become a territory. Congress made it wait for a variety of political reasons, but Yankton was the territorial capital for most of the vast area north and east of here for some time. So, there is much history here.

I took my supplies back to camp that now had more activity than seemed possible. It is not clear why fires burn at nearly every site all day. Since some people run out as soon as it is daylight, I suppose they cook every meal out there (lots of bacon, beef and brauts). Given the amount of wood that accompanies each group, I suppose it is easier than starting another in the evening. This day the weather is still pleasant enough although the humidity is rising and the south wind is blowing, which, the natives tell me, will bring more heat and lots of flies. I now share the van with many bugs: gnats, "no seeums", and others not known to me, but seemingly benign. Surprisingly I do not have any ants. The flies are becoming dense by nightfall. I realize that one of the weapons I forgot to buy or bring was a fly swatter, so the body count before my light goes out depended on my dexterity with a rolled up magazine.

The pleasant day ends watching this mass of humanity in the park settling down for the night while talking to my interesting neighbors from across the road. He is likely the most avid Notre Dame fan I have ever met. He is an electrician from nearby and has been here vacationing for a week. His fiancée, who is a college student majoring in computers and what seems like a number of other thing is equally as interesting when I can get her to talk. They will be married next year and seem a nice couple. I enjoy their youthful outlook on life and the belief that here in South Dakota almost anything is within their reach.

The rules say that quiet hours begin at 11 PM, and despite minimal patrolling by rangers, it does. Large groups of people sit by the fires on this warm night and "visit" without raising their voices. It would astound the police force at Coney Island, New York or the shore towns in New Jersey.

On Sunday it seems it is hot before the sunrise. It will get hotter. By 10:30 the park begins to empty. By noon, my neighbors are taking down their pop up trailer. These things that are about four feet off the ground when being towed have always fascinated me. They are high enough to stand in when fully cranked up and deployed. They sleep four normally, have water and electric connections, but are more like a tent than a trailer. My immediate neighbor and his wife and two girls were pleasant people who have apparently been doing this for some time. Watching them take it down is like watching a ballet. He never goes inside and she never comes out until it is ready to crank down. They do it very quickly and I apologized for staring, but I had never seen it done and certainly was impressed with their efficiency. He said they had been doing it since the girls were quite small and they found the ground a little harder than what they wanted to sleep on at night. His wife joined us to tell me that the temperature gauge in the truck was already near 90 degrees. I am told I can expect it to get hotter and likely stay that way all night since they knew of no weather fronts coming through.

Most of the vast area is empty soon after, some will spend the afternoon boating before they leave for Sioux City and Sioux Falls and the other populated areas, but some will start home and beat the worst of the heat. Tomorrow is a working day for almost all of these people. On Sundays, I sometimes have to remind myself of that now that summer is here and I see less of the "full time" RV crowd and more of the weekend campers. By 3 PM they are all gone, save three sites that are still occupied, although I seem to be the only one around. I will be here until Monday morning. It is disturbingly quiet, but peaceful. It is so hot, the van must be closed (with a substantial number of the flies in it) and the air conditioner turned on. By evening the heat is brutal, yet the television tells of heat in Rapid City (near my next destination) of 100 degrees or more with no relief due. I do not look forward to the 400 mile drive to Deadwood tomorrow at the other end of the state. When heat comes to the Plains there is no escape, the wind makes it worse and the only relief is thundershowers that may lead to a tornado or a fire. It can be a brutal land, just as it can be a postcard scene of rolling plains planted with grain and feed for cows and horses.

I sleep fitfully with the air conditioner roaring above my head. I leave earlier than planned and use the time to stay off the Interstate and see some of the small towns that I still, for reasons I cannot explain, find so charming and mysterious.

TWENTY-SIX

DEADWOOD, CRAZY HORSE, AND MOUNT RUSHMORE

I do not recommend a trip across the breadth of South Dakota in one day in the midst of a heat wave with high winds pushing your high profile camper from side to side. It is a long way and hard work since the stops are few.

The scenery is vast and, some would say, boring. I do not find it that way. I found the trip here from Yankton interesting. Early, I was on state roads moving through towns like Wagner, Amour, Winners and Stuckney. The full heat had not yet taken the day and the wind had not reached its' height in the furnace like conditions of the afternoon. These towns, many with fewer than 500 residents, bring thoughts of what it would be like to live here. There are small business districts in each— some much smaller than others—but the distances between them and even among neighbors seems huge to me. What does one do when this becomes frozen tundra? What of fire or the need for an ambulance? Are we so much less self reliant than these people? Or are we self reliant, too, only in a way that fits our circumstance? We can cope with traffic and smog and crowds. They admit they cannot but cope with great distance between towns and their neighbors with relative ease, which is something most city people would not do well. Still, I find this rural world where people actually do come from towns with less than 100 people fascinating. There is nothing multi-cultural, multi-racial or, in some cases even multi-family about them. Is it not homogenized milk? How is it possible to learn of a world where one will go, as the Mother of Mitchell did, to live in a place of competing wants, needs, ethnicities, and languages? It is hard for someone, who grew up only a few miles from the largest city in the country to imagine. There are no reference points; no way to say that it is "a little like..." for me there no are comparisons. I know from friends who grew up in such places that they feel they missed something, but also feel they gained something in values and hard work that perhaps we did not. I now see the towns and the land and I wonder again of the gain and loss.

As you drive the width of a state like South Dakota, you have time to wonder about many things like these. You speed along an Interstate, which may as well be any route for what little traffic it carries this blistering day in June, battling the fierce wind to remain on the road, in heat that will melt you when you stop. The flat prairie that surrounds you, is broken by a few things, most notably the hideous 300 or more billboards for the "famous" drugstore in Wall ("As written about in the New York Times Seven Times"; "As seen on the CBS Morning News"), it can seem a desolate place to some. Wall is a town that is the entrance to the Badlands. Apparently, many years ago, the proprietors of what then really was a Drugstore put up a sign on the highway offering free water. That was a big deal then. Wall is the turnoff you take if you want to really explore the Badlands the place where General Custer made his big mistake. It is now a huge store that has everything, or at least the signs would have you believe that. I felt it bore looking at only to see what kind of a place had that little respect for the environment, and would advertise for 300 miles for a one-stop customer. I circled the building, realized it was very crowded and about 100 degrees outside. I had my own water and my desire to see more vanished so I took to the road once again.

I later had a long and animated discussion with a fellow camper in Deadwood named Harry about the signs. He contended that if the signs weren't there that there would be "nothing else to look at" across the length of the state, so they were fine with him. I suggested that if the state wanted to be seen as the billboard heaven of the now known world that was its' prerogative, but perhaps they could consider putting up something that was worth reading, or just let me enjoy the scenery.

There is much, I found, that I never learned about this part of the Upper Midwest. Why, for example, do beef cows here chew grass in "herds" and not spread out on the hillsides as they do in the east and south? Perhaps it is a way to stay cool. Why do they bale the alfalfa (a city boy is told that is what it is) in rolls and sometimes leave it in the fields for more than a season? Why didn't I know there were so many horses here, more in some places than cows? There are Arabians and all manner of others. Why are there so many abandoned buildings along the way? Are these the family farms that have gone under that Willie Nelson and his friends have concerts to help? Are those little buildings which look like they will last awhile, but seem uninhabited, the famous "line shacks" where workers, too far from the main house to return each night, spend a week working on the fences? Why do the cows all begin to walk somewhere in single file around noon? Are they going somewhere for a more substantial lunch than the grass they have been chewing all morning? The grain elevators that appears on the horizon every 50 miles or so is a massive structure. It is the skyscraper of the plains, seen from miles away. Why is it tall and not wide? So many things I do not know that are obvious from the landscape if one looks. There is much food for thought here, yet in the cars that go by, napping and eating seem to be the preoccupation.

The prairie seems as if it will last forever until, quite suddenly, the Badlands appear. To an Arizona native, this area would look like home, except some of the smaller mesas have grass on them. My route takes me north of the most impressive ones, but the sight of these once again affirms that I am headed west, toward home. It seems a long time since I have seen a landscape like this.

I turn north just short of the 100 degree temperatures of Rapid City and begin to go up hill. The heat begins to lift. I trade altitude for degrees of temperature and at the end of a long drive it is welcome. To get to Deadwood, I pass through Sturgis, the site of the famous Harley Davidson Annual Rally for at least the last 60 years. It is not much of a town but for one week in August it is as crowded with as many motorcycles as anywhere on earth. Last year there were 300,000-500,000 people here. This year there may be a million or more. It is hard to imagine that something that began in the 1930's with a few people who wanted to race their old Indian model motorcycles could have grown so massive and attract so many people. This year there will be a television show about it (says the local newscaster) that will focus on the "Harley Women." Alas, I will miss it, but unlike my beloved ballparks, I will not regret it. I am told that a car I once owned attended while being driven back to San Diego after a sojourn in Washington D.C. A rather bizarre but incredibly bright fellow who worked with me drove it back to California and came through during rally week. He apparently lived in it for three days. More than that, I do not want to know.

Deadwood is even higher up and it is cool. By opening the windows, I make most of the flies disappear. I explore Spearfish Canyon Trail, which is indescribably beautiful with Bridal Veil Falls clearly the highlight for most. The falls are at least 20 stories high and the water comes so gently down the rocks from the crest of the hill, you can understand the name immediately. There is much more to see there. "Dances with Wolves" was filmed near here and there are some log homes along the way in the non-park sections that are remarkable. Spearfish Creek runs alongside the road throughout and has sluices and dams left from mining days.

I make my pilgrimage to Mount Rushmore. It is as impressive as anything I have ever seen. It is hard to imagine its' size when looking straight up at it. It is of such an enormous scale it seems it would be better viewed from several miles away. There are masses of humanity here now all with the latest in cameras and video equipment who also all seem to want to get into one of the largest gift shops I have ever seen. I go to several viewing platforms to be sure I have seen this massive work from as many angles as possible. The sculptor, Gutzon Borglum, started the work in 1927 at the age of 60 and was still at it in 1941. He had originally planned to sculpt the president's to the waist. Given the massive size of the finished work with only the heads there, it is hard to believe anyone could have been so bold to even think of such a thing. When he died, work stopped until his son took over and finished what you now see.

I stop at Crazy Horse, the dream sculpture of the Lakota Sioux. It is not a government memorial. I find that I missed Mrs. Ruth Ziolkowski's 91st Birthday by one day, but she is there when I am, entertaining visitors and, no doubt, raising money that the Federal Government doesn't give to this tribute to the Native American. That is because the family does not want to do it the way the "feds" want them to do it. They fear it will require them to have the parking garages and attendant clutter that now surrounds Rushmore. They are into natural things, not marble stairways and arches, or promenades of the states.

Begun by her husband Korczcak, when the Lakota Chief Henry Standing Bear summoned him in 1948, seven of his ten children have labored to finish this massive work still using the drawings and models he used. He worked most of his life on this tribute, not only to the Sioux, but also to all Native Americans. He came with $174 dollars, and it is said he had less when he died in 1982. It is amazing that so much work has been done, but even more dismaying is how much is yet to be done. Perhaps it will someday be finished. Estimates are, if no one loses interest, 75 years or more at the rate they are moving now. Maybe it will be sooner, as a result of Indian gambling. It will not likely be because the Congress will fund it unless the children lose interest or run out of money or someone gets greedy and lets the government do it their way.

I spend a full day driving 150 miles or more through the Black Hills National Park. There is the requisite amount of trashy commercial enterprise—reptile houses, caves of mystery, haunted canyons and lots of mines—long abandoned—to explore. There is even a zoo somewhere up there. But there is much beauty as well, more than there is of the questionable enterprises. One would find them anywhere near such wonders. Greed again, despoiling no more here than it does near Gettysburg or Cooperstown. I return to Deadwood, grateful for the cool of the evening air. The campground is well kept and is actually right in town, which is unusual. Deadwood is a gambling Mecca again, thanks to the Lakota this time. In its' heyday when it was known as Deadwood Gulch it harbored the con men and the gamblers of the old west. There is a trolley that comes up the hill every half hour to take any of us who want to lose our money down to the casinos. The old timers claim it was charming once when it still resembled a mining town, which was not so long ago. It has been discovered by the yuppies and is now considered quite chic. I do not find it so. Many of these rebuilt villages are and I like them. This one has the smell of money in it and crowds that shop and gamble until each day is over. New attractions are being built all the time. They are generally overpriced and not all that impressive to me, although the tourists seem to enjoy it all.

Tomorrow, I will leave this state of many faces, and I hope, the tourists who become thicker and ruder by the hour. Wyoming and Colorado beckon and decisions about where I go from there.

TWENTY-SEVEN

WHEATLAND, WYOMING

Today's drive of 260 miles began early to beat some of the heat. Traveling over the mountain and out of South Dakota retraced some of my tour of yesterday. Once across the border into Wyoming, the tourism is gone and the rural splendor of enormous ranches begins just as the heat returns. My route takes me west and south towards Cheyenne. I spend the day watching the deer, elk, and other wildlife roam freely through the fields with the cattle and horses. The deer and elk have no natural enemy here, not in summer when there is no hunting, so they forage along with the others. Wyoming is very dry this year. The fear of forest fires is very real and they have already occurred north and east of here. No open fires will be burning here tonight. I will not miss them.

I move through the empty countryside, through the towns of eastern Wyoming. I pass Redbird and Hat Creek, the Mule Creek Junction and Lusk before reaching Fort Laramie where I take my lunch and a tour. It is an incredible place in the history of this part of the west. The Original flagpole is all that remains, but it was an outpost for the white man deeply resented by the Native American that seemed to suffer constant attack, or whose soldiers were asked to ride to the relief of others over long distances in extreme heat and cold. There is a monument to a rider who was sent for help in three feet of snow. He traveled more than a hundred miles in two weeks through drifts as tall as he, and arrived on

Christmas Day to deliver his message to the Fort Commander. It notes that he died four days later and his horse died two weeks after that. This clearly was not a place for the timid or the faint of heart. Yet it seems so barren now, seemingly without reason to be so contested. But it was the place of the Bison herds then and important to the ranchers and settlers as it was as a hunting ground for the natives.

I had no idea how long this drive would be so I planned on a stop north of Cheyenne in a town called Wheatland, in what is described as a public campground. For reasons that still puzzle me, campgrounds are either scarce in this state, or they chose not to list themselves in the "bible" of Trailer Life. Since I am finding more than I read about I suspect it is the latter.

This is a "no reservation" public campground. The description is more than apt as it turns out. It is so public; it is in the middle of the town park. There are about 15 electric hookups available for a maximum stay of three days with even more tent spaces. There are four baseball diamonds just outside this park and it is also next to the city pool and tennis courts. It is as if you built a very small house under a shade tree in the middle of the town park. I have a seat for two of the games in left field this evening as Wheatland takes on someone. Meanwhile an American Legion game proceeds to my left and a women's softball game directly in front of me this afternoon. This is the leading vote getter for the most unusual campsite I have found thus far. It ranks up there with the one in Iowa next to the cornfield and the Interstate. There are three others of us here; eschewing the commercial park near the highway that has amenities but no shade and lots of traffic noise This rather idyllic small town setting seems such a wonderful idea. There are no fees, except what you may wish to give, electricity only at the sites along with picnic tables, and the park. It is a shame more towns do not provide such a site. It would be nice to have the choice to come off a highway every night to such a place nearly in the middle of the community rather than some of the more commercialized accommodations (or a night in a K-Mart parking lot). One of my fellow campers was surprised it was in the book and hoped that wouldn't make it too popular. He says that a number of the small towns throughout the Midwest have these sites and they are just not advertised. I hope I will find more of them. He stays here so he can walk to the golf course up the road about a mile. The folks of Wheatland get my vote for hospitality.

From here it is south to Fort Collins and then on to Littleton for the 4th of July with family. I will be off the road a week, and I will decide then where this odyssey will go next.

TWENTY-EIGHT

FORT COLLINS AND DENVER, COLORADO

The trip from Wheatland to here was quick but still hot. I have not been to Fort Collins for nearly twenty years. There are those I know here that claim it has not been this hot since the last time I was in town. It and the whole state of Colorado, for that matter is having one of the worst hot spells in awhile. Once here, it remained in the high 90's with no relief likely for the next two weeks. As I moved west I have had 90 degrees days or better since the last day in Yankton. It is generally not warm at night, particularly at these elevations, but it is tiring. It takes the zest I might have for touring many places along the way. There are still a number of National Parks I would like to see as I head west and south toward home, but if the heat continues, they will get but cursory looks and mostly from inside my van.

Heat, especially dry heat is not very kind to me. If I dehydrate, which is almost impossible not to do in this heat and lack of humidity, my blood pressure will become unstable and my general energy levels will be way down, so I am likely enjoying the heat even less than most others. I can remember a time when 90 degrees meant very little to me. Now I must protect against it, or it may take a day or two to get over it.

The trip down through Wyoming was on the "Curt Gowdy Highway." For you younger folks, he is a fellow who once was the

172

announcer for every important televised sporting event in the country. Now in his eighties, he is honored by the state where he starred at basketball at the University of Wyoming. In his time he was one the very best announcers in basketball, particularly, and close to that at football. Late in his career he seemed to confuse easily, forget names, and mispronounce them. It is only recently that I learned he was an alcoholic for a time and it likely ended his career earlier and more ignominiously that it should. He is better now and still lives in his beloved Wyoming where as a young man he first found fame and glory.

The landscape is stark. There are lots of mesas and ranches along the way. These are the smaller ones. That is, both ranches and mesas. They are of no consequence compared to those in the north or the east of the state.

Fort Collins is many things. It has a remarkable history little known to the non-natives who think of eastern Colorado as the place where Denver is and people ski. When the state first entered the Union, Fort Collins lost the ballot to become the capitol by one vote. It is the site of the Overland Trail. There is a road by that name there and yet few know that it follows the original trail for some distance. It is the trail used by so many wagons moving west that there are places where deep ruts remain made by the thousand of wagon wheels. It was a Fort in the beginning to protect the new white settlers against a variety of Indian tribes. Long before the west was well settled, it was an outpost for the lucrative fur trade for both the French and the English. The Poudre River runs nearby. It is now a place of kayaks and rafters as the waters are swift, but the name comes from a French word derivative and was used by early pioneers to bring there pelts down from high in the mountains each spring.

It is also the home of Colorado State University, which as many of the "State" schools, began as a teaching and agricultural college but now is arguably the best veterinarian school in the country and has many ecological and endangered specie grants.

I had the chance to get up into the Rocky Mountain foothills here along the Poudre River. There were lots of rafts and kayaks racing down. It is both fun and a way to stay cool. I was able to get close to the river and enjoy the cool breezes of the morning. By 2 PM it is too warm to stay unless you want to kayak.

On Sunday it was on to Littleton to spend a week off the road living in the driveway of more of my understanding family. My oldest nephew and his wife and their two children were the lucky ones this time. The two year old is new to me and I to her. She is a shy one at first, but a funny, indestructible one. Her older sister is still the drama student of the family. That and her ability to live without sleep are legendary. She remains the well-spoken little lady I met four years ago. The other is not far behind.

The 4th fell in the middle of the week, so I did laundry, caught up on family news, ate lots of good food, talked about all manner of things and was usually shown the driveway by about ten o'clock. It was cool by then, so sleep was easy. In fact there was very little hard about this week at all. As in Virginia and elsewhere, I enjoyed sleeping in my efficiency and spending the day in a real house.

I spent the 4th of July in the tradition of suburban America. A parade of children, adults in golf carts, miniature Harley Davidson's, and scooters of all description got it started. It ended for us by being able to watch the fireworks from the back patio of the house with a lot of the neighbors, which beats fighting through the crowds. A lovely day in good company.

The Fourth also brought the "webmaster", my brother's oldest son, and his bride out of the city to enjoy the festivities. We got a chance to visit and I to hand over some new pictures which would update the narrative that is appearing on the website. He is the technical wizard that has maintained it for the trip. He has posted the narratives and the pictures and made it interesting for the surprising number of people who have followed my progress. These are skills far beyond the capabilities of his technically impaired uncle and have been greatly appreciated by many others who have seen parts of this journey as their own.

I finally leave my gracious hosts as they begin a new week and soon, a real vacation for them with a trip to the east coast. They have been, as have the rest, most gracious to the weary traveler. There are storms on Sunday afternoon that bring temporary relief. The heat will be back, but by then I will have risen quickly to more than 14,000 feet as I go through the passes to the west and on to Vail, Aspen, and Snowmass. These names of winter already cool me, although I know I will then go on to Grand Junction, which, when last I looked, had a 97 on the thermometer.

I leave knowing that I have opted for a reasonably fast push toward home. The heat is in every direction and the tourists are getting thicker now that the Fourth has passed. Almost 50 per cent of the people of the country take their vacation in the next two weeks and I have no desire to compete with them for campsites and the "right" to have fun.

TWENTY-NINE

COLORADO AND UTAH

The morning began in Denver in cool air after yesterday's storms. I quickly moved up into the passes in the Rocky Mountains along Interstate 70. I reached more than 14,000 feet before noon and enjoy scenery like none other in the country, perhaps the world. I followed the Colorado River down the mountains' western slopes running small but wild here, with fly fisherman enjoying the pristine air and sky. The rafts and kayaks too, move down the quick water. The stream along the road passes golf courses on the other side of the water. It is a postcard, a time when these mountains release a frozen grip on the land and give it a look of a lazy area in the back county of San Diego.

The river remains to the left as I headed downhill and make my way to the western side of the state. The southern side of the road is lush and well irrigated by the river. A winery passes. Farms of all description flourish. But the north side of the road is arid land. It appears that the road either caused it, or is the ribbon of a bookmark that separates these different ecosystems that live in apparent harmony. The mesas to the right continue into Grand Junction at the western end of the state. The southern side eventually becomes the same.

Grand Junction is a much different town from those in eastern Colorado and those like Denver on the "Eastern Slope", of the Rocky Mountains. The Colorado River is here and just beyond in Utah I will find the Green River on its' journey south. This is how Colorado was, this town, before Denver became a place to live and base businesses, and before President Ford made Vail famous. It is hot here. Yet it is above 3,000 feet. It is the end of the Rocky Mountains and the beginning of the Wasatch Range that makes up so much of the beauty of Utah. Here they are stark and red, with spires larger than the Temple Joe Smith built there.

Unlike the mountains to my back, the land looks stark and forbidding here. There is a beauty to it but it is very different. There are signs announcing exits by number or as a "Ranch Exit." It is hard to see a ranch, in some cases impossible, but they are out there for this is a ranch town. The people are ranch people. The people are kind, but this is not a thriving area in the same way as the towns on the eastern slope. It is the west; it is not the urban west. These are cowboys, but these are the ones Willie and Waylon sang about. There are no urban cowboys in western Colorado.

The evening is warm; no rain threatens here although torrential rain falls but a few miles northeast near Provo and on the road to Salt Lake City. The morning will be as it is today and the weather in the part of Utah I am headed for appears even warmer. The heat is tiring, the air is thin, and one is often left breathless from simple tasks. The food at "Starvin 'Arvins" is not very tasty, but it bothers the cowboys less than me. They are friendly but distant, perhaps not sure of this stranger who now, by license plate at least, is not far from home. They have seen us all headed for the mountains. They are not impressed.

The morning is bright and turning warm early. Breakfast is better. The fuel is cheap. Life is good as it always is at the beginning of the new day. I am off for the brown Wasatch and the town of Richfield that looks on the map to be a short ride. It is not.

-2-

When routes back to California were discussed, this was both the quickest and the least desirable. The heat has added to that. Many of the National Parks within a day's drive have been eliminated because of it. This has put me in the tourist season where I least wanted to be. Do not misunderstand, I have nothing against people taking vacations, I just prefer to be elsewhere when they do since I do not have to take them when they do.

The distance to this destination in Utah does not seem far but I have learned long ago that whether the route goes up or down hill has a lot to do with how long it will take. A lesson never learned fully on this trip is that it may look short on the map, and would be, if one did not have to account for the elevation changes. The hills I have to climb are just as determinate of distance as the straight line. I make a short trip into Capitol Reef National Park as the heat lets me, but getting out isn't reasonable. There are only a few of us hardy souls up here and some are even out looking at the strange formations in this Park that the early settlers thought of as barriers to any route to the south. Despite these short side trips it is more of an Interstate trip designed to get closer to home than a sight seeing one. It is one that takes concentration to even stay aware of the scenery.

The arid country does not yield much in they way of interest. The off-Ramp signs now only have numbers. There is a sign that warns that there are "no services" for the next 100 miles. Then, as I move through this land that seems so vacant and desolate, towns begin to appear and the interchanges begin once again to have fuel and food at the cloverleaf. A motel or two appears. For many miles now, I have see trucks simply pulled up onto the off-ramps where I presume the drivers are catching naps before the heat gets too intense and after a long night's drive. Now there are places for them and the RVs and cars to huddle together once again and ice tea can be had and I can sit and wonder where all these young women come from with their small children to meet other young women for lunch. It is a foreign concept, "doing lunch" at a Denny's at the edge of the Interstate. Or it is foreign to me. I wonder mostly where they live since signs of houses are still rare. But along with the rest of us they huddle at these oases in the desert.

Soon I begin to descend and green becomes a color again as the waters that feed the Green River nourish the land. The town of Green River is the demarcation point that is the most noticeable. I drive through it mainly because I am amazed it is there in some ways and to learn a bit more about it. The Green and the Colorado are the major rivers that flow south from up here and they join further south. It is a unique town in the history here since Major John Powell put to rest the theory that there was no way south beyond the "Reefs" above. He was a civil war veteran who left here with ten men to map and explore the Green and Colorado Rivers. He provisioned for 100 days and, against the advice of about everyone, he left in May. One man left the trip the next day and two others deserted shortly thereafter. He eventually reached a downstream settlement in July. Two years later, with three boats and more men, he managed to navigate most of the upper Colorado as well. The Shivwit Indians were settled here but had never attempted the feat. They did kill the two men who deserted on the first voyage, but Major Powell's accomplishment likely led to the wide belief that the Greene and Colorado Rivers were not just the wild streams they appeared to be here, but very navigable waters that could be used for commerce.

The green ends here again as quickly as it started and the Wasatch Front Range is next. The brown and the heat are still there. In the late afternoon, some isolated storms overtake us and cool the air as we reach Ritchfield for the night. It is a pleasant town that caters to those of us who are moving through to Colorado or north to Salt Lake and Park City. The night is pleasant. Again I forsake camping for a motel room. I decided coming out of Denver that unless it got a great deal cooler, I would do so on my last three nights before home.

It rained heavily during the night and again the mornings starts well and cool enough to enjoy. I reach the western end of Interstate 70 and turn south on Interstate 15. If I stay on this long enough, it will take me to within twenty miles of my house. I will make one more stop in St. George, Utah. It is just north of Las Vegas. Since I have no desire to be in Las Vegas, St George is the only choice. A weather report tells me that it will be over 100 there today. I have spent the morning wandering around and the heat is back so I head for town, hoping that the motel will give the weary traveler an early check in time.

-3-

This town was not very much even a few years ago, but it is becoming substantial now as place to retire for those from California and else-where. Its growth has been a sprawl on the sides of the mesas. Some of the homes look and are quite expensive. The town in the valley has grown large and quickly to keep pace.

It appears that many of us have decided that the motel is preferable to both camping and continuing. There are three campsites in and near the town that I pass. None are full. The motel has a large number of people milling around in the lobby, which is strange for 2:30 in the afternoon. The clerk assures me that my room is ready. I ask of these others. They are, as I had suspected, pilgrims of the road also looking for an early check in time and not a group holding a conference here today. I am able to get my room early because no one used it last night.

I am thankful for that. I move the van to the rear where I will be able to get the luggage in more easily and notice that the car wash has a temperature sign. It says 116 degrees. It is, of course in the sun, but so am I and it is as warm a day as I can remember. The cool quiet halls of the motel make great sense. A quick trip across the parking lot to a diner for lunch is about all I can manage before I fall to reading and trying to finish as much of my electronic log as I can. I am glad to be off the road and glad that tomorrow will bring me home.

THIRTY

COMING HOME

The last day on the road was a blur. It was hot, it was in heavy traffic, and it was all on a familiar part of Interstate 15. It was the antithesis of what the trip had been about. Still, it was mindless driving through familiar territory that gave me time to reflect on all the days and nights and states and towns I had been privileged to see. I can say that my zeal for documentation may have been eroded, but the good feeling I had when I left that early April morning was still with me. I never lost my enthusiasm for the trip. Whatever ambivalence I had when I left disappeared. I look forward to seeing my house fill the windshield again, but I am not at all sorry I went.

John Steinbeck in his book, *Travels with Charlie,* wrote that he knew the journey was over, when it just did not matter anymore. A road was a road and a face was a face and a conversation was best carried out in monosyllables. He said he could not remember anything about driving to New York after a particular stop he had made in Virginia. He just drove until he got home. He did not care what or who he saw. I think if there was a moment like that for me it was the day I pulled out of Utah.

It was just a drive. There is nothing pretty about it. I was back in the desert. There was no wonder left. I was as bloated with information as a sponge is with water. But that was the last day. I do not know what would have happened if it had come much sooner. All I had to do was drive home in about six hours. I felt for Steinbeck. That was a long way to go with no interest in the going.

Strangers and friends had shared thoughts and insights with me. There is also now a group of people I never knew before with whom I hope to stay in touch who did the same. There are others who shared their wisdom but not their hometown and, in many cases, not even their last name, in the campgrounds and along the roadsides, who will never know how much they meant to the trip.

My family and friends thought this worthwhile. I appreciate that encouragement found mainly in the absence of rejection of the idea as stupid or impossible now that it is over.

Some find it strange that someone in my condition does such a thing. I do not, but it is clear from the many comments I have collected over the course of nearly 11,000 miles that many do not share that view. If I had a nickel for the number of times that I had to articulate a response to a variation of the question: "You aren't alone, are you?" it would likely make good my stock market losses over the last 12 months. Most people, quite without malice or thought, do not expect to meet a person with a serious mobility impairment out in the world alone. I do not know why we are all supposed to have companions. In most things in daily life they are not necessary. They are not, I was sure, necessary to me in my ability to take a van across the country and back, while living in it. There also were many people who "got it". They did not find it extraordinary and it gave me great pleasure to meet them and share the journey.

This trip was a very small sample of a strip of the country that I passed through. It does not pretend to be anything more than that. It represents what a diverse place that part of the country is. I found people in the middle and on both coasts far more alike than different in their hopes and dreams for themselves and their children. We are an odd country. We all see each area or state or region as "different" when what I saw was a similarity that surprised me. The mayor in Oklahoma had his hopes for his family and his town. The lady who worked in the

Town Hall in Milan, Ohio had hers. Even my gracious friend Dot had a life she enjoyed and lived fully. So too, Buddy and Boots. They each express it in a different way but they all hoped for a decent life and a tomorrow more prosperous.

I was humbled by the grandeur of so much of what I saw. I was in awe of The National Parks, of the monuments, and the natural beauty of a summer morning in the Wyoming countryside or the Smoky Mountains or the plains of South Dakota, or a sunrise on the beach in Connecticut or a sunset on a lake in Oklahoma. I was most impressed however, by so many people who seemed to truly care about themselves their neighbors and me. The amount of trust and a willingness to help and share that is still out there is astonishing.

The young children of my family charmed me. They are so young and innocent and happy. It pleases me that I was allowed to get to know them, or, in some cases, to know them again. I am proud of my nieces and nephews who have taken on the world and still have time for their families and other people. They work hard to care well for their families. This trip gave me the chance to enrich my relationships with them and store new and wonderful memories I will enjoy in more reflective moments.

I saw the small towns that I set out at first to try to understand, but later realized were not understandable to me. The people who live in them are, in their core beliefs and emotions, no different than those of us who live in or on the fringe of the huge metropolises. We enjoy living here, and they enjoy living there. It takes a special skill to endure in their environment that is different but no less intense than it does to endure in ours. They would not change places with us, nor would most of us with them. I am still fascinated by their way of life, but I am not surprised that they enjoy it. Given time, I might learn to do so as well.

I am as healthy as I was when I left. I did it the way I wanted to do it. I think it was a true "Victory Lap." There will be other trips but this was the one that proved it could be done. I saw friends and family and remembered how much I care for them all, and met new people and realized I still have the capacity to care anew.

Parts of the trip were scary and uncertain, but mostly, the random acts of kindness committed by strangers helped me find a way. It also affirmed for me that retiring from a life's work does not mean there are not other challenges. It does not have to be dull, or safe, or certain. One need not become an old man in shiny pants eating macaroni out of a tin plate with a wooden spoon watching television reruns. Somehow, this trip proved there is more to it than that for me, I hope, for many years to come.

There are pictures in my mind and conversations shared and stories about places I have been and people I met that will be memories I will cherish forever.

EPILOGUE

The trip on which this book is based began in April of 2001. It ended in July of the same year. It does not take into account what occurred in the United States in September of that year and thereafter.

It is about the people who refer to themselves as "Americans" who are really citizens of the United States of America that I met and had the chance to get to know. It is not about terrorism and does not reflect their views about it. Terrorists were not high on the list of what most of us thought about then, although, in hindsight, perhaps we should have.

I am sure that these people think more about it now. I know that the people in New York, New Jersey and in the Washington, DC area think of it a lot. For some there is the time before and after that tragic day in September. It is a line in their lives that is indelible. I am not sure that those in the heartland all draw that stark distinction. Those I have been able to talk to since the trip are more aware of foreign affairs now, but I do not believe they have much changed their own lives except to feel less secure.

So the book remains a story of a man and a victory lap, not tainted by subsequent events. I do not believe that all experience before that date need be colored by the events since. Many of those I saw and mention here were affected, some grievously, by those events, and they horrified us all. But in most of the places I went the people have gone on pretty much as before. They admit to now being more aware of the world and the fact that there are people in it that hate the United States and what it stands for. Yet they still have time for conversations like we had, the laughter we enjoyed, and still show the kindness they did then. To forget what life was like in the spring of 2001, or to judge it based on subsequent events, would be unfair.

Mine was a whimsical trip through the United States by a man in a van sampling the people and places that I found there. That it took place before September 11, 2001 does not make it less valid. It is still the trip of an ordinary man taken under extraordinary circumstances who expresses his thoughts about what he sees along the way. Some things have changed since I was there, but, having been back to some of the places since then, on the whole, my belief is, most have not. That is the spirit in which the book is written. It is not social commentary; it is a narrative work of non-fiction. It is, I hope, an interesting story.

0-595-25346-6